Timothy Dalton's James Bond
- The Retrospective

John Fox

© Copyright 2021 John Fox
All rights reserved.

Also by John Fox:

No Time to Die - The Unofficial Companion

Contents

5 - Preface

9 - Chapter One

24 - Chapter Two

33 - Chapter Three

48 - Chapter Four

60 - Chapter Five

68 - Chapter Six

82 - Chapter Seven

91 - Chapter Eight

101 - Chapter Nine

114 - Chapter Ten

125 - Chapter Eleven

133 - Chapter Twelve

143 - Chapter Thirteen

152 - Chapter Fourteen

PREFACE

In 2006, with the lingering fallout of Die Another Die still attracting stray remaining brickbats, a more grounded and thoughtful reboot of the James Bond franchise arrived to great acclaim when Casino Royale was released. Daniel Craig, making his debut as Bond, was lauded as the first actor to take the character seriously, tone down the flippant humour, and give 007 any sense of an inner life. I can't have been the only Bond fan at the time rather puzzled by this thesis. Had everyone completely forgotten about Timothy Dalton? Dalton had already done all of those things in 1987 and 1989! "Funnily enough," said the former Bond director John Glen in 2012, "looking back at the two films that I did with Timothy Dalton, The Living Daylights and Licence to Kill, I find him to be quite similar to the new Bond (Daniel Craig). He and Daniel are both harder-edged Bonds. I think Timothy was before his time. You look at Licence to Kill now and it keeps up. It's more in vogue now than when I shot it, I think."

There is sometimes a general perception (or at least was for a long time) that Timothy Dalton was an absolute disaster as Bond and nearly sank the franchise. This perception is a consequence of the fact that Licence To Kill struggled in the amazing North American blockbuster summer of 1989 and also because Dalton only made two Bond films. This general and simplistic perception of Dalton overlooked a number of mitigating factors though. Licence To Kill did perfectly fine outside of the United States and Dalton would have made a third film in the early 1990s were it not for litigation which eventually kept James Bond off our cinema screens for six years. If these legal woes had not transpired, Dalton probably would have made about four Bond films - which would now put him on par with Pierce Brosnan.

One other factor we shouldn't forget is that Timothy Dalton got plenty of praise when The Living Daylights came out for making Bond more realistic and down to earth again after the

Roger Moore films. It was only really in the wake of Licence To Kill and Dalton's official departure in 1994 that a revisionist take on his era began to paint him as a hopeless failure. A strange phenomenon with James Bond actors is that their Bond tenures seem to be more harshly judged once they no longer have the role and are consigned to history. Sean Connery, as the original and most would contend the best, was of course immune to this retrospective 007 reappraisal curse.

Timothy Dalton was lauded in 1987 for trying to make the Cinematic Bond more faithful to Fleming's Bond. Nowadays though, an unquantifiable number of people still wrongly tend to assume that Dalton must have been dreadful because he only made a couple of films. Roger Moore made more James Bond films than any other 007 actor but you'd think he was awful and unpopular in the part if you read half the retrospective articles about the James Bond movies. It is very fashionable to trash the Roger Moore era and yet the Moore era was highly successful and actually brought countless new fans to the franchise because his films were fun and very entertaining. The biggest victim of retrospective reappraisal is surely Pierce Brosnan. Brosnan was deemed pretty much the perfect person to be Bond in 1994. Martin Campbell said that Pierce Brosnan playing Bond in Goldeneye was such a no brainer that he didn't even want to test any other actors.

Few seemed to have any obstreperous complaints about Pierce Brosnan from 1995 to 2002. And yet, when Brosnan was replaced and suddenly became an ex-Bond, he was retrospectively judged to have been terrible in the part. One suspects that Brosnan simply caught some 'friendly fire' in the end because of the diminishing artistic returns of his Bond movies. You can't really blame Pierce Brosnan for Die Another Day not being Goldfinger. The writers, producers, and director of Die Another Day were the ones to blame - not Pierce Brosnan. It will be interesting indeed to see what the retrospective consensus on Daniel Craig might be in several years time when he is merely an ex-Bond and someone else is established in the part. Craig may or may not elude this

strange retrospective James Bond jinx. We shall see.
The debate though over eras, actors, and films is the beauty of the Bond series. We all have our own likes and dislikes - whether conventional or unconventional. Some fans love Timothy Dalton's darker and more brooding take on the character. Some fans love the tongue-in-cheek humour and fun of the Roger Moore films. Some fans love the 'rough diamond' Bond of the Daniel Craig era. And some fans love all the eras - warts and all. I do sense that history is at least starting to becoming a little kinder to Timothy Dalton's James Bond in recent years. It could be that the Daniel Craig films have played a not insignificant part in this. Maybe people have looked at the Daniel Craig films and suddenly realised they are not a million miles away from what Timothy Dalton was gamely trying to do back in the late 1980s.

'For me the name is Dalton, Timothy Dalton, wrote Gwladys Fouché in the Guardian Film Blog in 2006. 'He was dark, he was ruthless, and he managed to show precisely what Bond was all about: a merciless, calculating, professional assassin. Is it inappropriate to mention that he was also unbelievably good-looking and charismatic? So why is he still treated as though he massacred the role? Timothy Dalton was a great 007. Ironically, the very characteristics that got Dalton slammed are the very same things that the Bond producers are praising Daniel Craig for. On and on, they have said they want Bond to be closer to the original Ian Fleming character. They want him to be grittier, darker and less jokey. What they really want, it seems, is to have Dalton back.'

I find my own appreciation for Timothy Dalton's contribution to the Bond franchise and his two movies increasing year by year. It's been nice too to see him emerge again in recent times as a rather cultish actor thanks to things like Doom Patrol, Hot Fuzz, and Penny Dreadful. Happily, it seems that Dalton's time as Bond, for so long lazily dismissed as some sort of misstep or wrong turn in the franchise, is also now beginning to get the retrospective praise it richly deserves. I actually think Timothy Dalton in The Living Daylights might be the best James Bond we've ever had. I'm sure many might disagree with that assertion but that's the fun of being a Bond fan. We all have our own personal opinions and views to venture forth with and debate.

In the book that follows we will take a look at the history of Timothy Dalton's relationship with the James Bond franchise from his early days as an actor (amazingly, Dalton was a potential Bond candidate as early as 1968) through to his eventual casting. We'll also take a good look at his Bond films from their production to release and see what worked and what didn't. This book will also look at the various plans for a third Timothy Dalton Bond film and examine why Dalton left the role in the end. Most of all, this book is a celebration of Timothy Dalton's James Bond. So, without further ado, let's begin telling the incredible story of the most underrated Bond of them all...

CHAPTER ONE

Timothy Dalton was born in Colwyn Bay, Wales, in 1946 to an English father, Peter Dalton Leggett, who was a captain in the Special Operations Executive during the Second World War, and an American mother named Dorothy Scholes who was of Italian descent. Dalton left school in 1962 at 16 to enrol in the Royal Academy of Dramatic Art and tour with the National Youth Theatre. He grew up in Lancashire and his native regional accent (though tamed over the years by his training as an actor) can be rather charmingly detected in Licence To Kill when Bond tells Franz Sanchez that "things were about to get NASTY." In 1966, Dalton appeared at the Royal Court Theater to play his first lead in the National Youth Theater's production of Little Malcolm And His Struggle Against The Eunuchs.

In 1967, Timothy Dalton appeared in the fourteen part television series Sat'day while Sunday. This was an ABC series about young people in the north of England. It ran for fourteen episodes and the cast included a young actor named Malcolm McDowell. This show is incredibly obscure and was only ever broadcast in a few regions. Years later, Dalton was asked about Sat'day while Sunday in an interview and said he honestly couldn't remember anything about it at all. After some early television roles, in 1968 Dalton made his film debut as Philip II of France in The Lion in Winter (based on the play by James Goldman). Peter O'Toole, the leading man in the film, had recommended Dalton to the producers after watching him in the theatre.

The Lion in Winter won three Oscars (including one for Katharine Hepburn as Best Actress) and was a success at the box-office - grossing over $22 million from a $4 million budget. The film also marked the film debut of Anthony Hopkins and Hopkins and Dalton became good friends through their experience of making the film together. Decades later, there was even an attempt to cast Hopkins in Dalton's elusive third Bond film. A combination of The Lion in Winter and his impressive stage work brought Dalton to the attention of the James Bond producers and casting agents - who at the time faced the unenviable task of trying to find a replacement for Sean Connery in their lucrative Bond franchise.

The James Bond film franchise (based of course on the popular series of spy thrillers written by Ian Fleming) is a very special and unique series quite unlike any other. When it began in 1962 no one could have possibly dreamed of the success and longevity it would enjoy. There had been franchises before Bond - like Tarzan, Sherlock Holmes, Charlie Chan, The Falcon, Jungle Jim, Frankenstein, Lassie, Rin Tin Tin, Bulldog Drummond, Hopalong Cassidy, and many others. As the Bond series began, thrifty but fun franchises like Godzilla and the Carry On films were already becoming popular in their respective countries.

The Bond franchise created by producers Cubby Broccoli and Harry Saltzman however was completely different. Previous film series operated strictly on the law of diminishing returns and lowered the budgets accordingly. They sought to extract every last penny out of their licenced property without actually spending any money. The Bond series reversed this tradition. Each new Bond film was bigger than the one that came before. More lavish, more expensive, more spectacular. It was a gamble that paid off handsomely. Adjusted for inflation, the most successful James Bond film of all time is 1965's Thunderball. Thunderball marked the peak of sixties Bondmania but the series would still go on and on with enduring success and seemingly without end.

Cubby Broccoli and Harry Saltzman needed a new James Bond for 1969's On Her Majesty's Secret Service and their casting people believed Timothy Dalton, who was darkly handsome and rather Byronic, might be worth a look. However, Dalton felt that at twenty-four he was far too young to to even consider play James Bond. Though invited to a OHMSS casting call, Dalton didn't bother to turn up. More than anything it was the thought of having to replace the seemingly irreplaceable Sean Connery that made Dalton spurn any chance (however remote - he was simply invited to a casting call and never offered the part) to throw his hat into the ring.

"When Sean Connery gave up the role," said Dalton, years later, "I guess I, alongside quite a few other actors, was approached about the possibility of playing the part. That was for OHMSS. I was very flattered, but I think anybody would have been off their head to have taken over from Connery. I was also too young. Bond should be a man in his mid-30s, at least - a mature adult who has been around." Dalton was a Bond fan and said he had watched the Sean Connery films in the cinema. His favourites were the first three - Dr No in particular. Dalton preferred the fairly restrained nature of the early films to the gadget festooned extravaganza approach of something like You Only Live Twice. The irony of this is that On Her Majesty's Secret Service would turn out to be the most human and Flemingesque Bond film of all.

After a very extensive and highly publicised casting process, a twenty-nine year-old Australian named George Lazenby was eventually cast as the first non-Connery James Bond. Lazenby, unless you count a Big Fry chocolate commercial, wasn't even an actor. He had rather blagged his way to an audition by pretending to be a playboy and actor. "I had no acting experience," said Lazenby. "I was coming from the male model point of view. I walked in looking like James Bond, and acting as if that's the way I was anyway. And they thought, 'All we have to do is keep this guy just the way he is and we'll have James Bond.'"

Despite his inexperience when it came to acting, Lazenby was very impressive in his Bond auditions and he certainly looked the part. Lazenby was up against John Richardson, Hans de Vries, Robert Campbell and Anthony Rogers in the final Bond auditions. John Richardson, the lean blue-eyed star of One Million Years B.C, was briefly in pole position and quite close to getting the 007 role but Lazenby moved things back in his favour when he accidentally broke the nose of stuntman/wrestler Yuri Borienko with a wild punch during the fight scene part his audition. George Lazenby seemed like someone who could handle himself in a real fight and this obviously impressed the Bond people.

On Her Majesty's Secret Service did reasonably well at the box-office but critics and audiences couldn't help but miss Sean Connery. It should be noted though that Connery had grown tired of the role (the absolute apex of Connery's annoyance with all things 007 is said to have famously arrived when a fan tried to follow him into the toilet for an autograph while he was shooting You Only Live Twice) and probably wouldn't have mustered much enthusiasm for OHMSS even if he had somehow been lured back. Besides, one of the strengths of the film was that Lazenby's youth and inexperience gave him a vulnerability which wouldn't have been so believable if conveyed by Connery's Bond. Oddly enough, Lazenby, though an inferior actor, actually suited the more human story of OHMSS more than Connery.

Given that George Lazenby was only five or six years older than Timothy Dalton, Bond fans have sometimes wondered if Dalton could have actually pulled off OHMSS at the time. He was clearly a better actor than Lazenby and had the requisite dark good looks. It's hard though not to disagree with Dalton's own view that he was far too young to be a realistic James Bond at this time. Lazenby, although only in his late twenties himself, did have a fairly mature (and very 1960s) sort of male model Milk Tray Man look which meant you never questioned his age.

Strangely, it's not that difficult to watch OHMSS and just accept this is still Connery's Bond with a different actor - and the film is determined to run with that concept, even linking the title sequence into the Connery films. Lazenby was chosen because of his physical similarities to Connery. As with Connery, Lazenby was also believably tough and had a rough and ready sort of quality. A 24 year-old Dalton, though his performance may well have been excellent, would have been less believable as a direct continuation of the Bond established by Sean Connery. Timothy Dalton never really tried to copy anyone when he landed the part of Bond whereas with OHMSS it's obvious that the producers were trying (for the most part) to broadly mimic the Connery Bond template with Lazenby. Dalton in OHMSS would be like a fine vintage opened too early. His time was bound to come.

After George Lazenby declined an invitation to return as James Bond in Diamonds Are Forever, he was frozen in time as the 'one-off Bond' and it was often wrongly assumed that both Lazenby and OHMSS had been a failure. Over time though, the strengths of the film have been rightly acknowledged. The film was rare in the Bond franchise in that it was a relatively faithful adaptation of a Fleming novel. This meant that OHMSS had an amazingly downbeat and bold ending for a Bond film. It is arguably the most human Bond film ever made and also has beautiful Alpine locations, the peerless Diana Rigg, fantastic action sequences, and a wondrous John Barry score.

One could plausibly argue that On Her Majesty's Secret Service is the best James Bond film EON have ever made. In 2013, the film director Steven Soderbergh went into bat for OHMSS and argued this very case when he said - "Shot to shot, this movie is beautiful in a way none of the other Bond films are — the anamorphic compositions are relentlessly arresting — and the editing patterns of the action sequences are totally bananas; it's like Peter Hunt took all the ideas of the French new wave and blended them with Eisenstein in a Cuisinart to create a grammar that still tops today's how fast can you cut aesthetic, because the difference here is that each of the shots — no matter how short — are real shots, not just additional coverage from the hosing-it-down school of action, so there is a unification of the aesthetic of the first unit and the second unit that doesn't exist in any other Bond film. And, speaking of action, there are as many big set pieces in OHMSS as any Bond film ever made, and if that weren't enough, there's a great score by John Barry, some really striking sound work, and what can you say about Diana Rigg that doesn't start with the word WOW?"

George Lazenby naively presumed OHMSS had made him a star and that he would now go off on his merry way as a successful and much in demand actor. However, much to his dismay you'd imagine, Lazenby was suddenly plunged into absolute obscurity. A 1971 drama about gun runners called Universal Soldier (in which Lazenby played a hippie mercenary in London) was partly funded by Lazenby but completely bombed. Lazenby spent the rest of the seventies making cheapie Hong Kong action flicks and Australian television movies. George Lazenby had failed to deduce the simple and universal fact that no actor was bigger than James Bond. Lazenby assumed he was a star after OHMSS but James Bond was the star. By leaving the Bond series after one film, Lazenby stupidly pressed the self-destruct button his own acting career before it had even begun.

George Lazenby had wrongly assumed he would be awash with offers. The problem for Lazenby though is that he wasn't an actor. His performance in OHMSS, guided by the director Peter Hunt and the supporting class of Diana Rigg, was remarkably good given his inexperience. But he had no acting career to fall back on. Aside from a Big Fry chocolate commercial, Lazenby had no acting CV at all before Bond. Sean Connery, Roger Moore, Timothy Dalton, Pierce Brosnan, and Daniel Craig were all professional actors when they were hired as Bond. They all had, to varying degrees, a body of work (Connery was actually the most inexperienced out of the five because he was only 31 when he became Bond) behind them and a career to fall back on. Lazenby was never willing to serve his apprenticeship - something that the other Bond actors all had to do before they became rich and famous.

The most remarkable thing about Lazenby's departure from Bond is that he genuinely seemed to believe he was leaving a sinking ship. His agent Ronan O'Rahilly told him that James Bond was conservative and out of vogue. A dust shrouded relic of the fifties that would wheeze on for a couple more films and then be consigned to cinematic history. It was one of the stupidest pieces of advice anyone could ever be unfortunate enough to receive. Many decades later, Lazenby could probably allow himself to see the funny side as he signed autographs at Bond conventions and did yet another interview about his time as James Bond. Fads and eras (not to mention actors) come and go but James Bond was indestructible and forever. Lazenby had to learn that lesson the hard way.

The interesting thing about On Her Majesty's Secret Service is that it showed the Bond formula was more flexible than might have been suspected. Compared to gargantuan tongue-in-cheek extravaganzas like Thunderball and You Only Live Twice, OHMSS was surprisingly dramatic and emotional. It presented Bond not as an indestructible superhero but as someone who could have his heart broken. OHMSS was the first film in the franchise that explored the concept of making Bond more human. However, whether it was the box-office (which was decent enough but a considerable drop from You Only Live Twice) or the fallout from Lazenby affair, the producers were in no rush to repeat the experiment. It would be seventeen years before the Bond franchise attempted to make Bond more human again.

In 1970, Timothy Dalton appeared in the BBC production Five Finger Exercise. He then appeared in the historical film Cromwell and also played Heathcliff in Wuthering Heights. He followed this up with an appearance in the Italian film Giochi Paticolari - where Timothy suffered the indignity of having all his lines dubbed. 1971 found Dalton in Mary, Queen of Scots alongside the likes of Vanessa Redgrave, Trevor Howard, and Glenda Jackson. Mary, Queen of Scots found Dalton with blond hair giving a rather theatrical performance. He still seemed too callow and fresh faced to be a James Bond candidate at this time. It took Dalton a while to grow into his wolfish good looks.

Meanwhile, George Lazenby's sudden and unexpected departure meant that the Bond producers had to find another new James Bond for 1971's Diamonds are Forever. Timothy Dalton does not appear to have been a candidate for this film - and still doubtless considered himself far too young to be considered for the most famous role in cinema. As ever, a large number of actors were auditioned, approached or interviewed for the role of James Bond in Diamonds Are Forever. They included Michael McStay, Simon Oates (who said he thought he had the part at one point - his agent was negotiating a fee with EON), Clint Eastwood (who definitely wasn't interested), Roger Green, Peter Anthony, Adam West (yes, Batman!), and Burt Reynolds. "Cubby Broccoli came to me and said - We want you to play Bond!" said Burt Reynolds. "In my stupidity, I said - An American can't play James Bond, it has to be an Englishman. No, I can't do it. Oops. Yeah, I could have done it and I could've done it well."

Roger Moore (a man always on the EON radar) was not in contention for Diamonds Are Forever because he was tied to a television contract on The Persuaders. In what was considered to be a surprising decision, the American actor John Gavin was eventually signed by Broccoli & Saltzman to play Bond in Diamonds Are Forever. Gavin was best known for playing Sam Loomis in Psycho and a Bondish spy in O.S.S 17 Double Agent. Gavin was certainly handsome but a bit wooden. "Time was getting awfully short", said Broccoli of Gavin. "We had to have someone in the bullpen."

United Artists were not enthused at all by Gavin and decided to go all out to get Sean Connery back. This required the studio to pay a then unheard of fee amounting to $1.25 million (which Connery donated to charity), support two film projects of Connery's choice, and also pay the actor compensation for any overrun in the weekly shooting schedule. It was a sensational deal at the time and illustrated that as far as United Artists were concerned the Bond franchise was simply not viable without Sean Connery. The unlucky John Gavin was compensated financially by the studio for the termination of his contract and drifted into television roles. In 1981 he became the United States Ambassador to Mexico.

Diamonds Are Forever saw a big lurch in tone towards tongue-in-cheek humour after the more sombre and tragic events of On Her Majesty's Secret Service. While purists might have been dismayed by this shift to a more campy and flippant type of Bond film, from a commercial point of view it made sense and the flaws in the movie were mitigated by the delight audiences felt at Sean Connery's return. The plot of Diamonds Are Forever is vague to the extreme and some of the special effects are strangely mediocre for a James Bond production (the satellite set-piece is atrocious) but the feeling of aimlessness that seems to dog Diamonds Are Forever is compensated for by some fun escapism - like the oil pipe sequence, Bond's fight in the elevator, the Las Vegas car stunt (where the Mustang famously comes out of the alleyway the wrong way up), and the large scale oil rig battle sequence at the end.

Sean Connery is clearly coasting in Diamonds are Forever. He's a little bit pudgy and has the air of a man who is impatient to get back to the golf course. However, he is of course terrific muttering the deadpan quips supplied by Tom Mankiewicz. The film has an enjoyably surreal atmosphere at times with the desert sequences and the famous Moon Buggy setpiece (Bond encountering a 'moon landing' in a television studio seems to be an early reference to those conspiracy theories that the moon landing was hoaxed). The score by John Barry is appropriately strange and makes a nice sonic backdrop for the action. One of the disappointing things about Diamonds Are Forever though is that it barely mentions the events of OHMSS (where Blofeld and his goons murdered Bond's wife). Despite the return of Connery, part of you wishes Diamonds Are Forever was a direct follow-up to OHMSS with Lazenby.

Diamonds Are Forever, with its humour and camp (Blofeld

resorts to drag at one point), set the tone for the seventies Bond films to come. You could argue that Diamonds Are Forever feels a lot like the first Roger Moore film. Despite the best efforts of United Artists, Sean Connery decided that Diamonds Are Forever was definitely the end of association with James Bond - until 1983 at least. He had grown weary of the role in the 1960s and found the fame and attention increasingly constrictive. As Connery pointed out, The Beatles had their fame spread over four people whereas with the James Bond craze it was him all on his own.

Sean Connery found it increasingly tedious portraying the same character all the time and was eager to play new roles. Connery always seemed happy and liberated to play against his Bond persona. The Anderson Tapes showed that Connery wasn't afraid to look his age and explore new roles. The Offence and Zardoz, which both followed Diamonds Are Forever, were ample proof too that Connery was tired of Bond and ready to move away from that image. Although it was a coup to get Connery back for Diamonds Are Forever, United Artists were simply delaying the inevitable. Sooner or later an actor capable of making the Bond series viable without Sean Connery would have to be found.

In 1972, Timothy Dalton was cast in Robert Bolt's film Lady Caroline Lamb but then replaced at the last minute. Dalton took legal action (and won his case) but the film still went ahead without him and he was replaced by Jon Finch. Finch (like Dalton, a brooding young actor known for Shakespearean roles) was felt to be a hot rising star at the time and destined for great things so he was presumably deemed more of a coup to hire than Dalton. Timothy Dalton was not finding it easy to carve out a film career at all. He had already been passed over for roles in big films like Cabaret and The Battle of Britain. Somewhat disillusioned, Dalton now decided to turn down all film offers (which included a part in Richard Lester's The Three Musketeers) and spend the next three concentrating on stage work.

"When I was in my 20s," said Dalton, "I'd had a lot of good successes. I'd done The Lion In Winter, Mary Queen of Scots, Wuthering Heights - playing any parts. Rightly or wrongly, and I think I was influenced by peers and colleagues around me who had been involved in filmmaking or stardom, and then disappeared. I actually wanted to learn my craft. I wanted to be an actor all my life. I love writing, I love the work, I love my job and I knew I was a beginner. I also felt that I wasn't ready to be playing leading parts with Katherine Hepburn, Peter O'Toole, Alec Guinness, Richard Harris, Glenda Jackson, Vanessa Redgrave, Ian Holm. I felt, in a way, that I didn't deserve it, so I knocked it all on the head. I turned every movie down and went into three solid years of theater, because I wanted to improve; I wanted to learn and really develop. I was wrong, because only young people can play young parts, and it was young parts I was playing, and I think I was playing them very well. But I know I'm a better actor because I went back to learn."

It seems plausible to venture that Timothy Dalton's decision to turn his back on films for a while came from a fear of being typecast. Dalton, because of his anachronistic good looks and stage background, seemed to be constantly cast in costume dramas. Even at this tender age in his career, Dalton must have been starting to wonder if he would ever be offered anything else! While going back on the stage exclusively for a period did allow Dalton to decompress and master his craft, his profile did unavoidably diminish somewhat as a consequence. It meant that his chances of becoming a film star became more remote at this point. The unusual thing about Timothy Dalton though is that he didn't really seem to care that much. He was never someone who chased after fame or money. Dalton simply enjoyed being an actor.

While Dalton went back to the theatre, The James Bond franchise began yet another search for a new leading man. Now that Connery was gone (again) a new 007 actor was required for 1973's Live and Let Die. Once again, EON began testing, interviewing, and approaching actors who might potentially have the right stuff to become the new James Bond. The actors approached or tested for Live and Let Die included John Ronane, Julian Glover, David Warbeck, Jon Finch (who turned them down flat), William Gaunt, Patrick Mower, John Richardson (again), Jeremy Brett (later to become famous on television as Sherlock Holmes), Guy Peters, and Michael Billington.

In the end the Bond producers settled on a familiar face to become the third official James Bond. They decided to cast Roger Moore. Moore had been considered for (what became) OHMSS and probably would have been approached for Diamonds Are Forever had he not been tied to a television contract at the time. After the Lazenby affair, the Bond producers did not want to risk casting another unknown or inexperienced actor and they calculated that Roger Moore would be a safe pair of hands to steer the franchise for a few pictures at least. At 45, Roger Moore was the oldest actor to win the role of James Bond but - strangely enough - in Live and Let Die he could pass for the youngest! He looks incredibly boyish and youthful in the film at times.

Roger Moore was already well known to audiences because of his television show The Saint. His Bond tenure was rather like The Saint on a much bigger budget. Moore's time as Bond wasn't exactly radical but it was fun. Roger Moore went on to make seven films (a record that is unlikely to ever be broken) and proved that the Bond franchise was a perfectly viable ongoing commodity even without Sean Connery. The Bond franchise, with periodic recasting of the lead, could potentially go on forever. As George Lazenby will tell you, James Bond is much bigger than the actor who happens to be playing him. It is a brand as famous as any in cinema. James Bond is completely indestructible.

Live and Let Die was a restart for the series after the studio and producers finally accepted they would have to go on without Sean Connery short of kidnapping him. George Lazenby was chosen because of his physical similarities to

Connery and given the tropes of the cinematic Bond (tuxedo, casinos, Dom Pérignon etc) but Roger Moore was a different kettle of fish. It was the franchise that had to change to accommodate Moore - not the other way around. Roger Moore was more lightweight than the actors who came before him but more urbane and refined. Moore is not the most physical actor but he's more plausible in Live and Let Die than Connery or Lazenby as someone who would know his way around an outrageously expensive wine list or designer wardrobe.

Though he might not quite have been everyone's cup of tea, Roger Moore proved to be an excellent custodian of the Bond series and the box-office success of The Spy Who Loved Me and Moonraker at the end of the seventies found the franchise in rude commercial health. There was a slight hiccup early on in the Moore era when The Man With The Golden Gun met with a lukewarm reception in 1974 and shortly after co-producer Harry Saltzman left the franchise because of financial difficulties. The Spy Who Loved Me, destined to arrive in 1977, was seen as a make or break film for Cubby Broccoli and marked a return to the epic extravaganza Bond pictures of the sixties like Thunderball and You Only Live Twice, with incredible fantastical sets by Ken Adam and lavish photography.

The Spy Who Loved Me cost twice as much as any previous Bond and the money was on the screen. It felt like a big and ambitious film compared to many previous - and subsequent - Bond entries. This was the picture that firmly established Roger Moore as James Bond. The next entry in the franchise (Moonraker) attempted to cash in on the Star Wars craze (although, strangely, Moonraker's most common touchstone is actually Kubrick's 2001 rather than Star Wars) and took James Bond into space. While purists felt the Roger Moore films were becoming too outlandish and that the comedy was beginning to get out of control, there is no question that this approach was popular with audiences at the time. By the end of the seventies, the Bond films were a million miles away from the approach that Timothy Dalton's casting would later demand.

It was at the end of the seventies when Timothy Dalton got another brush with potential Bondage (if you'll pardon the expression). Dalton seemed to be very much on the radar of Cubby Broccoli. Broccoli always kept a close eye on the male acting pool in Britain lest he should need a new Bond again. Truth be told though, Cubby was naturally a loyal and conservative man when it came to casting. The Bond films were doing perfectly well at the box-office with Roger so Cubby saw no reason to make a change if he could avoid it. When there was a mild uncertainty over Roger Moore's future participation in the franchise after Moonraker, it appears that Timothy Dalton was someone that Cubby Broccoli had on his list of potential replacements. However, Dalton was apparently not that enthused by the prospect at the time.

"There was a time in the late 1970s," Dalton later confessed in the book The Incredible World of 007, "when Roger may not have done another one, for whatever reason. They were looking around then, and I went to see Mr Broccoli in Los Angeles. At that time, they didn't have a script finished and also, the way the Bond movies had gone - although they were fun and entertaining - wasn't my idea of Bond movies. They had become a completely different entity. I know Roger, and think he does a fantastic job. He was brilliant. Roger is one of the only people in the world who can be fun in the midst of all that gadgetry. But the movies had gone a long way from their roots; they had drifted in a way that was chalk and cheese to Sean. But in truth my favorite Bond movies were always the first three."

Meanwhile, Timothy Dalton had continued to spend the seventies working on the stage and modestly carving out a career in film and television. Strangely though, despite his dashing good looks and acting chops, Dalton never really threatened to become a star in the seventies. He appeared in Play For today, a Dirk Bogarde espionage caper called Permission To Kill, and an obscure Spanish film called The Man Who Knew Love. By the end of the decade, Timothy

Dalton's screen career seemed to be going no where in particular. He infamously appeared in the eccentric Mae West megabomb musical comedy Sexette. His other roles included the TV miniseries Centennial and Dalton also appeared in the popular TV show Charlie's Angels as the dashing Damien Roth.

The one bright spot was Agatha - a decently reviewed 1979 drama about Agatha Christie's famous 11-day disappearance in 1926. Dalton played Archie Christie in a cast that included Dustin Hoffman and Vanessa Redgrave. While Timothy Dalton still flew somewhat under the radar in the 1970s this would not be the case in the next decade. Dalton would land the two biggest roles of his career in the 1980s. In 1980, he took his most famous and enduring role outside of James Bond - that of Prince Barin in Flash Gordon.

CHAPTER TWO

Flash Gordon is a fantastic 1980 science fiction adventure film directed by Mike Hodges and based on Alex Raymond's vintage comic strips. Timothy Dalton had moved to the United States at this point in his career in an effort to find more screen roles but he was more than happy to return to Britain to make Flash Gordon when he was offered the part of Prince Barin. Dalton had actually watched Flash Gordon serials at the cinema when he was a boy and he loved the completely overblown style of the film when he arrived on the set.

"I'm astonished by what a huge cult film it is," said Dalton in 2014 of Flash Gordon. "But I have to say that the Americans didn't get it at all at the time. It's taken maybe 30 or 40 years to realise it's a joke! I loved being in that movie! I try and love being in every movie I do. It's such a waste of time if you're not in love with the movies you do. Not only is it a waste of time, it's a waste of effort if you're not in love with the movies you do. I've only got one or two that I've not been particularly enamoured with once I've started. But in general, you've got to love what you do. And you've got to communicate that you love it. But Flash Gordon I just thought was a fabulous film, and as I say, I was disappointed, but now I laugh about the fact that it was, I think, the second highest-grossing film in the world that year and it bombed in the United States!"

The story in Flash Gordon begins with Emperor Ming the Merciless (Max von Sydow) and his chief crony General Klytus (Peter Wyngarde) amusing themselves by provoking natural disasters on Earth ("An obscure body in the S-K system, your Majesty...") at the push of a console button. Meanwhile, New York Jets American Football star Flash Gordon (Sam J Jones) boards a private plane as the weather takes a disconcertingly strange and ominous turn, meeting travel journalist Dale Arden (Melody Anderson) onboard.

With storms raging all around them due to Ming's distant

shenanigans, Flash and Dale end up crashlanding in a greenhouse/lab belonging to Dr Hans Zarkov (Chaim Topol), a mad scientist who believes that this bad weather is coming from somewhere out in space. Zarkov has been building a rocket to locate the source of this unknown trouble and he manages to get Flash and Dale onboard before he launches them all into orbit. Although they don't know it yet, their destination will be the planet Mongo where Emperor Ming and one of the most colourful adventures in cinematic history await.

Flash Gordon is enjoyably, ridiculously overblown and colourful, a film that knows it is ludicrous but doesn't really seem to care. It's Star Wars in a gigantic glitter dusted seventies disco with spangly fetishistic costumes, fantastically garish opulent sets, and an outrageous colour scheme (an awful lot of red and gold) that could grate cheese at a hundred paces. One thing I really love about Flash Gordon is that it places the budget up on the screen for us to see - Dino de Laurentiis clearly from the Cubby Broccoli school of filmmaking. It begins in winning fashion too with stills of the vintage Flash Gordon comic strips and the famous theme song by Queen after an early taste of Ming and General Klytus. Any film that teams up Ingmar Bergman's favourite actor and Jason King as the villains surely deserves some sort of award.

Once thrown into Ming's dastardly clutches (where the Fu Manchu-esque villain rules the galaxy from Mongo in grand and theatrical fashion) our hero Flash (who helpfully wears a t-shirt with "Flash" written on it in case we should forget who he is) soon begins a rebellion which will need the help of the reluctant Prince Barin (Dalton of course) and Prince Vultan (Brian Blessed). "Prince Barin! I'm not your enemy, Ming is! Let's all team up and fight him!" The only trouble is that Prince Barin takes an immediate dislike to Flash when his slinky girlfriend - and daughter of Ming - Princess Aura (Ornella Muti) takes a shine to the plucky Earthman.

Sam J Jones, who apparently had his voice dubbed, is not

Albert Finney, just as Melody Anderson (essentially Lois Lane without Margot Kidder's comic timing) is not Meryl Streep, but the variable acting almost becomes part of the charm in Flash Gordon. There is great fun to be had in counting the familiar faces in this picture. A pre-Bond Timothy Dalton (looking like Errol Flynn and Tony Stark from the Iron Man comics) making a dashing and earnest Prince Barin and Brian Blessed with his booming voice and trademark beard having the time of his life as Prince Vultan. Vultan is the leader of a group of flying Hawkmen, nicely deployed for the big battle sequence at the end. "Onward my brave Hawkmen! Let this be known forever as Flash Gordon's Day!"

Timothy Dalton seems to be having fun too, especially towards the end when Barin gets to run around shooting people with laser guns shouting things like "You bloody bastards!" or some such. I suspect that Edgar Wright's love of Dalton comes as much from Flash Gordon as it does James Bond. Dalton is so matinee idol handsome he even manages to survive wearing a silly Robin Hood type costume - although who doesn't have a silly costume in this?

The cast of Flash Gordon is hugely enjoyable beyond the serviceable leads. Max von Sydow is given some fantastic costumes and some marvelous comic book villain dialogue to dispense. "Pathetic earthlings! Hurling your bodies out into the void, without the slightest inkling of who or what is out here. If you had known anything about the true nature of the universe, anything at all, you would've hidden from it in terror." Peter Wyngarde is also fun as General Klytus - who he makes one of the campest and most sarcastic baddies ever to grace the screen. Klytus has a metallic mask that makes him look like Dr Doom and he has some amusing lines too. "Now, he showed promise!" he comments while viewing a Hitler speech via Zarkov's memories (which he is attempting to erase so they can use him as an agent).

Topol is good vale as the eccentric scientist with plenty of scenery to chew and Ornella Muti - who I can't believe never did a James Bond film - is memorably feline as Princess Aura with some of the skimpiest costumes ever to adorn a family film. Even Rocky Horror Show/Crystal Maze legend Richard O'Brien pops up playing a flute as Fico, one as Barin's men. Flash Gordon is full of scenes that everyone remembers - like the fight between Prince Barin and Flash on the booby trapped disc in Vultan's Sky City kingdom and the test that Flash must undergo on Barin's gloomy woodland abode (the forest moon Arboria) by placing his hand Russian roulette style in tree stumps where a very nasty poisonous creature may or may not await. We see none other than former Blue Peter presenter Peter Duncan illustrate what can happen if you pick the wrong stump.

Clearly some (camp) liberties have been taken here with the character of Flash Gordon but there are some nods to the strips and famous serial featuring Buster Crabbe with the planet backgrounds and some of the rocket ships. Cliffhanger situations abound and there are one or two close escapes for our hero (although you perhaps never quite get enough of a sense of danger with the tongue-in-cheek tone of the film). Logic is a not a major concern here but the lavish production design and sense of fun more than makes up for this. There are some wonderful matte designs and a big old-fashioned battle sequence at the end with flying Hawkmen, laser fields and the enjoyably anachronistic rockets. Flash Gordon is a feast for the eyes and wonderful entertainment. It is one of the greatest cult films ever made.

Back in the world of James Bond, it appeared that - briefly - the role was up for grabs again at the start of the 1980s. The concept of the 'reserve Bond', that is to say an actor who is on the EON payroll and ready to step into 007's shoes at the drop of a vodka martini, is something that was real in the Cubby Broccoli era. Michael Billington, a square jawed and hairy chested actor best known for Gerry Anderson's UFO and The Onedin Line, was used by EON to play 007 in screen tests for prospective Bond actresses in the seventies and early eighties. Billington was very nearly cast as Bond in Live and Let Die but lost out to Roger Moore.

Billington was then given a part in the PTS of The Spy Who Loved Me as Sergei Barsov, the lover of Soviet agent Anya Amasova. Billington was more or less an employee of EON and ready to step into 007's shoes at any moment should there be a problem with Roger Moore. Roger and Cubby would usually have some wrangles over Roger's salary for each new film before Roger (usually at the last minute) signed on the dotted line so Cubby liked to have a plan B up his sleeve. Michael Billington was Cubby's plan B for much of Roger's era.

When they were preparing 1981's Bond adventure For Your Eyes Only, Roger Moore's participation was not set in stone so Michael Billington was flown to Corfu (one of the locations for the film) and given a full costume test. In the end though, Roger Moore did the picture and Billington wasn't needed. Billington said that the same thing happened with Octopussy a few years later. Once again, Roger Moore decided to come back and Billington wasn't required in the end. Billington later said that when he saw the scenes in Octopussy where Bond is dressed as a circus clown he was rather relieved that he hadn't ended up in the film.

The late New Zealand actor David Warbeck also claimed that he was something akin to a 'substitute Bond' during the Cubby era. Warbeck, who was a sort of a cult B-movie action and horror star because of the many films he made in Italy, almost became James Bond in the early 1980s when the director John Hough was hired to develop a Bond film. Hough had made a film called Wolfshead (aka Wolfshead: The Legend of Robin Hood) with Warbeck and Cubby Broccoli decided that David Warbeck would be a sensible choice as the new 007 because he knew John Hough. In the end though, Roger Moore, as ever, decided to come back and his return dashed Warbeck's Bond dream.

Besides Billington and Warbeck, EON looked at any number of actors as potential replacements for Roger Moore in the uncertain period leading up to the production of what became For Your Eyes Only. These included Nicholas Clay (who was Lancelot in John Boorman's Excalibur), Patrick Mower (again), and Michael Jayston. One of the most popular candidates at this time to become the next James Bond was Lewis Collins - star of The Professionals on television. Collins was keen on becoming Bond and wanted to make the 007 films more like the books. "It would be nice to get back to the original Bond," said Collins, "not the character created by Sean Connery - but the one from the books. He's not over-handsome, over-tall. He's about my age and has got my attitudes."

If you watch the highly eccentric and daft but strangely entertaining 1982 action film Who Dares Wins (where Lewis Collins plays an SAS soldier) you can form a fairly good impression of how Lewis Collins would have played James Bond. Collins was not the world's greatest actor but he was terrific at playing terse, self-deprecating action characters. Lewis Collins would most likely have dialled back the overt humour and made Bond more plausibly dangerous again. Collins would potentially have been like Timothy Dalton - only without the subtext and depth. Lewis Collins as James Bond probably could have worked quite competently circa 1981.

It wasn't to be though. Cubby Broccoli is said to have taken an almost instant dislike to Lewis Collins when they had a meeting and that was obviously the end of any Bond hopes the actor might have harboured. "I was in Cubby Broccoli's office for five minutes," said Collins, "but it was really over for me in seconds. I have heard since that he doesn't like me. That's unfair. I think he's really shut the door on me. He found me too aggressive. If Cubby couldn't see I was being self-protective I don't have faith in his judgment."

Roger Moore, as ever, took all the 007 interviews and auditions in his stride. "To be honest I did want to make another film," he later said. "This was all part of the bargaining ploy on EON's side - let it be known they were testing others so

I'd take the deal on the table for fear of losing the part. Fair enough, we all enjoy a game of poker. I'm quite principled about not undervaluing my worth. If someone wants me for a job then I believe they should pay me a fair fee. My agent usually haggles it up a bit, the producer usually haggles it down a bit and a happy middle ground is found. If someone undervalues me, I simply walk away. I have no qualms about it."

On the basis of his meeting with Cubby Broccoli in the late seventies, it is plain that Timothy Dalton was someone EON would have seriously considered in 1980 had Roger Moore not come back. The evidence suggests that Michael Billington and David Warbeck were in pole position though. Many Bond fans feel that 1981 might have been the perfect time for Timothy Dalton to inherit the Bond mantle. In this scenario, Dalton would have been very much the eighties Bond and could have made five films. Dalton was about 36 around the time For Your Eyes Only was being prepped and fresh from the exposure of Flash Gordon.

With a few modifications, it is not that difficult at all to imagine Timothy Dalton in For Your Eyes Only. The film is fairly low-tech and eschews the space age gadgetry of the previous couple of Bond pictures. For Your Eyes Only is deliberately down to earth because the producers were sensitive to criticisms that Moonraker had been too silly and overblown. Because it was not known if Roger Moore was coming back, For Your Eyes Only was written in a rather generic way when it came to James Bond in the film. The opening scene where Bond places flowers on his wife's grave was written to connect a new Bond actor to the history of the franchise. This scene would have suited Dalton perfectly.

The keel-hauling sequence and the mountain climbing climax of for Your Eyes Only are also setpieces you could easily imagine in a Timothy Dalton Bond film. Things from For Your Eyes Only you can't imagine in a Dalton film are Lynn-Holly Johnson as Bibi Dahl, Victor Tourjansky's comedy cameo as the drinking tourist, Janet Brown's comic cameo as Margaret Thatcher, and Bill Conti's disco score. Imagine if you will though, For Your Eyes Only shorn of these elements and given a John Barry score. It might well have made a pretty solid debut film for Timothy Dalton in an alternative Bond universe.

One of the cast members of For Your Eyes Only was the Australian actress Cassandra Harris as Countess Lisl von Schlaf. Harris had recently got married to a young Irish actor named Pierce Brosnan. At the time, Brosnan's credits only amounted to small roles in The Long Good Friday and The Mirror Crack'd. During the production of the film, Cassandra Harris introduced Brosnan to Cubby Broccoli and Broccoli immediately made a mental note of Brosnan as a potential future Bond. Brosnan was dark haired, tall, very handsome, and very charming. Cubby thought that if Brosnan could polish up his acting skills he'd make a perfect James Bond in the not too distant future.

In the end, Roger Moore did inevitably return and made not just For Your Eyes but also Octopussy and A View To a Kill. Once again though the familiar game of poker over Roger's fee led to more Bond auditions before the cameras rolled on Octopussy. Olivier Tobias and James Brolin were both tested. At one point, Brolin (who would have been the first American to play Bond) was so close to getting the part that he began searching for a house in London.

Once again Michael Billington, as we noted, was still waiting in the wings too and ready to go on like a substitute striker in the last five minutes of a big football match. Cubby Broccoli even toyed with the idea of offering Superman star Christopher Reeve the part of James Bond in an effort to jolt Roger into signing a contract. US Magazine asked its readers in 1983 to vote for who they thought the next Bond should be. The poll was won by Pierce Brosnan in a landslide with 46% of the vote. In second place with 11% was Lewis Collins. Other names who earned votes from readers were Tom Selleck, Ian Oglivy, and Mel Gibson.

Meanwhile, as Cubby and Roger played out their last games of bluff, Timothy Dalton's matinee idol good looks led him to be cast in a number of undemanding playboy, romantic, or period roles. Sins with Joan Collins, Florence Nightingale, Chanel Solitaire, and Jane Eyre. The Doctor and the Devils saw Dalton forced to don period costume yet again. Despite a smattering of sporadic movie roles, Dalton was in danger of becoming a television miniseries actor. His real love still seemed to be theatre and in the early eighties he took to the stage in Henry IV, Part 1 and Henry IV, Part 2 with the Royal Shakespeare Company. Despite the success of Flash Gordon, Dalton had remained a very private person who didn't seem especially interested in fame.

CHAPTER THREE

At 57 years of age, Roger Moore finally hung up his tuxedo for good after 1985's A View to a Kill. It was high time to make way for a younger actor. 1984, the year before Roger's last Bond film was released, had seen a number of rumours that Pierce Brosnan was going to be the new Bond. An Australian newspaper published an article in which they said Brosnan had already signed a secret deal to replace Roger. Brosnan had to deny these rumours and even wrote to Cubby Broccoli assuring him that these stories did not originate from him or anyone connected to him.

1987 would mark the 25th anniversary of the James Bond series and what better way to celebrate than to launch a new era which looked to the future? The Bond producer Michael G. Wilson felt that the series needed to make some radical changes to stay fresh and relevant after seven Roger Moore films. Wilson drafted a treatment which was essentially an origin story. Wilson's script treatment had a twentysomething Bond teaming up with a veteran agent to battle a Chinese warlord named Kwang. By the end of the story, the veteran agent is dead and Bond has inherited his mantle and become a full fledged secret agent. The story would show us how Bond met M, Q and Moneypenny for the first time.

According to CinemaBlend, this treatment '... would have introduced the world to Lieutenant James Bond as he lives a carefree youth of punching out Austrian diplomats and gambling away what's left of his family fortune. Bond's grandfather and aunt are introduced at the Bond family's ancestral home, with James deciding to take up M's invitation into her majesty's secret service after his grandfather's passing. Learning from his mentor, 00-agent Bart Trevor, we eventually learn that Trevor recruited Bond into a mission to kidnap/kill a warlord known as General Kwang required someone with his skills on a short notice.'

The reboot story would have seen Bond travel to Scotland to explore his roots (something which EON clearly put in the bank and used for Skyfall) and end with him being asked to investigate Dr No. A DC3 aeroplane sequence in the treatment later seemed to end up in the 2008 film Quantum of Solace. It is pretty obvious that this treatment, had it gone ahead, would not have featured Timothy Dalton - who was nearly 40 at the time. This story would obviously have required a Bond actor in his twenties.

Michael G. Wilson's reboot script treatment (which was obviously an influence on Casino Royale in 2006 - though Wilson has downplayed this connection himself) was vetoed by Cubby Broccoli in the end. Cubby felt that audiences would not want to see James Bond depicted as a youthful amateur. He wasn't sold on the idea at all and preferred a more business as usual approach where Bond is a mature professional in his thirties or forties. Cubby was though willing to accept that changes would have to be made to the franchise to keep it fresh. He wanted the next film to be more grounded and feel like more of a blood relative to Ian Fleming than many of Roger Moore films had been.

It was decided that the next film would be called The Living Daylights. The Living Daylights took its title from Octopussy and The Living Daylights - the fourteenth and final James Bond book by Ian Fleming and published posthumously in 1966. There are four stories in this slim volume - two of which were added in later additions. The first two stories (Octopussy and the Property of a Lady) contained some elements which were used in the 1983 Roger Moore film Octopussy.

Octopussy concerns a murder victim called Hans Oberhauser who is found frozen in an Austrian glacier. James Bond is sent to Jamaica to talk to the last man to see the victim before his death. This just happens to be a certain Major Dexter Smythe. Bond is personally involved in the case as Oberhauser was a mentor to him in his younger days after the death of his parents. This short story was also an influence on the controversial Blofeld twist in the Daniel Craig film Spectre. The last story in the collection is 007 in New York. 007 in New York is a mildly interesting trifle that consists of Bond's general musings about New York and also a lot about food and where he will go to eat.

It was the third story that inspired the title and some elements for 1987's The Living Daylights. In this story a British agent known as '272' is heading back to the West through Berlin and the Soviets are sending their top assassin - codenamed 'Trigger' - to shoot him as he makes his way across no-man's land. M sends James Bond to kill the KGB assassin and 007 hunkers down in a safe house with his sniper rifle waiting for a shot at his target. What appears to be a female orchestra go in and out of the building Bond is keeping watch on.

Ian Fleming's The Living Daylights revolves around Bond's distaste for killing - despite it often being an unavoidable part of his job. This story would be incorporated into the beginning of the 1987 Timothy Dalton film of the same name in faithful fashion and presents us with a more weary, tired Bond who is questioning his profession and the things he has to do in the name of Queen and Country. There is a decent twist in Fleming's story when the target is revealed and the main drama comes from Bond's reaction to what he has been asked to do.

The constant on the writing team in the Cubby Broccoli era was Richard Maibaum. Maibaum and Michael G. Wilson wrote the screenplay for The Living Daylights together. You never really got too much script chaos on the old Bond films (although the screenplay for The Spy Who Loved Me went through many hands) because Cubby Broccoli liked everything to be planned out in advance. Maibaum said that the key to writing a Bond film was to come up with the villain's 'caper' first and then the rest would fall into place. If Cubby didn't like a script he would ask for more 'bumps' to be added. This was essentially his code for more Bondian staples. "Where are the bumps?" he would ask if the story wasn't sufficiently drenched in enough cinematic 007 residue for his liking.

It is sometimes reported that The Living Daylights was originally written for Roger Moore but this was not the case. Maibaum and Wilson knew that a new actor would be coming in for the next film. The identity of that actor proved to be a rather complex and circuitous puzzle to solve though. Cubby Broccoli thought he had solved the latest James Bond casting riddle when Pierce Brosnan officially signed on to play 007 in The Living Daylights. Cubby had obviously not forgotten meeting Brosnan on the set of For Your Eyes Only and kept tabs on him. Brosnan had begun his 007 costume fittings and shot a gunbarrel intro for The Living Daylights when fate intervened in very cruel fashion.

Brosnan's NBC (and produced by MTM Enterprises) television show Remington Steele - a piece of eighties fluff that had Brosnan as a suave pseudo private eye - was ailing in the ratings and on the way out but the studio decided to cash in on the publicity surrounding Brosnan and James Bond and optioned a new series just as Brosnan's contract was about to expire. NBC offered to adjust their Remington Steele schedules so Brosnan could still do The Living Daylights but Cubby Broccoli declined to take advantage of this offer. In those days television had less prestige than it does today and Broccoli simply didn't want to share his Bond actor with a TV show.

Broccoli had apparently told NBC they could have Brosnan for six episodes but NBC insisted on 22 episodes so no compromise could be arranged and EON decided to move on. "James Bond will not be Remington Steele, and Remington Steele will not be James Bond," declared Broccoli. The decision to 'reactivate' Remington Steele had had equally frustrating consequences for Brosnan's co-star Stephanie Zimbalist, who played Laura Holt in Remington Steele. Zimbalist had been cast as Officer Lewis in Paul Verhoeven's Robocop but had to abandon the film and go back to making Steele with Brosnan. She was replaced in Robocop by Nancy

Allen.

"My first reaction," said Brosnan, "was to tell them to shove the Remington contract. It was a knife in the heart. And not just for me, for my family, because we moved our children back to England and got ****** over by very short people. They had me by the short and curlies and there was absolutely nothing I could do. They'd nailed me to the wall. I went out and played a lot of tennis - to get the anger out of my system. You get over it. It's just being an actor."

The August 1986 issue of People Magazine featured Pierce Brosnan on the cover with the headline - Take This Job & Shove It. Brosnan was still fuming to say the least. 'Pierce Brosnan,' wrote People, 'the man who would be 007, finds himself behind the eight ball as he reluctantly returns to Remington Steele. "It was", says Pierce Brosnan, "too much like a job." Admittedly a good job, with more than good pay. In a series that made an obscure Irish actor into an American TV star. With a role that painted him debonair and slightly devilish. And an image that made him the perfect, obvious, only choice to become the next Bond, James Bond.

'Although Brosnan had prospered as the roguish title character on NBC's detective series Remington Steele, "I had just had enough," he says. In fact, "I'd had enough after two years, but I'd signed a seven-year contract." Brosnan was relieved -- "really relieved" -- when Remington Steele was cancelled last May. But wait. Put the emphasis on the past tense: was cancelled, was relieved. For just when it seemed that Brosnan had snagged one of the most sought-after and profitable roles in movie history, he now finds himself once again tied to Remington Steele, and he is not pleased.

'For most of the last two months, Brosnan thought he had fulfilled an ambition of long standing, to replace Roger Moore as 007. He had settled in London. Thinking he had closed a chapter of his career, he had taken to occasionally trashing Remington Steele and the high life in L.A. He had all but signed for The Living Daylights, the $40 million Bond film originally scheduled to begin shooting this month. Then, ironically, the prospect of Brosnan as Bond revived NBC's interest in its show. The network saw a promotional windfall in beaming the man who would be Bond into America's living rooms -- particularly after more than 10,000 furious fans phoned and wrote NBC protesting the cancellation.

'This summer, Remington has greatly improved its ratings during reruns. In the halls of NBC, programming chief Brandon Tartikoff joked about his booboo, "Anybody can cancel a show in 59th place. It takes real guts to cancel one in ninth place." Consequently, just last month, three days before options on the Remington cast expired, NBC made it official: The show was renewed for six episodes as a midseason replacement. Since then, the legendary producer and protector of the James Bond film properties, Cubby Broccoli, has been making like Dr. No. Although he had been negotiating a three-picture deal with Brosnan, Broccoli didn't want his 007 tainted by television. "He's not going to have another company riding on our publicity," says a Broccoli aide.

'To accommodate the movie's schedule, MTM, the production company responsible for Steele, even suggested shooting the season's first episode in Europe. "Obviously it would be to our benefit to have Pierce playing Bond, and we're not giving up on the idea," says Steele executive producer Michael Gleason. "Anything we can do, we are more than willing to do." But Broccoli has remained decidedly cool to stopgap measures. The net result for Brosnan is a career catch-22: Because Remington was cancelled, Brosnan could do Bond. But because he might be Bond, Remington was uncancelled. And because Remington was uncancelled, Brosnan may not be able to be 007. The choice for Brosnan seems clear: Bond or bondage.

'The network's decision has started a worldwide scramble for another Bond, while shooting on The Living Daylights has been postponed to late September. The producers talked to 60 aspirants in one recent week alone. After Broccoli saw The Taming of the Shrew in London, new rumors surfaced last week that actor Timothy Dalton was the first choice. If you are a handsome, breathing male with a British accent, you are a candidate. Brosnan has not talked publicly about his dilemma since Remington's revival created it. But he was positively voluble when last interviewed in London, basking in the afterglow of what he considered a pro forma screen test for Bond--and in the midst of filming a kind of warm-up for the part, Frederick Forsyth's thriller The Fourth Protocol, in which Brosnan plays a KGB bad guy.

'"Had Steele been renewed", he said, "I would have risen to the occasion, but I would have gone back to work reluctantly, just gritting my teeth. Under the circumstances [of the Bond offer], if it had gone a fifth [season], I would have been p***** off." For Brosnan, television was no longer the most becoming medium. "You learn bad habits as an actor [on TV]. As the season goes on, you take short cuts, fatigue sets in. Then your confidence goes." With it goes some measure of esteem. "The word 'star' doesn't mean an awful lot to me. 'Good actor' and having the respect of one's peers means more. You don't really get much of that doing a show like Remington Steele."

'By the end of last season, Brosnan wanted to leave Los Angeles as well as the show. Despite the comforts of a home in the hills, "I was becoming so Hollywood. All it became was money--get as much as you possibly can. I just find that you can become a very boring person living in L.A. I tell you, living there on a day-to-day basis is vacuous, terribly fake." So he particularly liked the prospect of shooting back-to-back features in London: "It's extremely civilized working here".

'Brosnan has long considered playing Bond a career goal, but only recently has he pursued that prospect with passion. In fact, when he was first mentioned as a candidate he was reticent. "I said, why do I want to do it? It's become an institution." But the idea kept coming back. Roger Moore told a newspaper that Pierce was his hand-picked successor. The mushrooming attention made Brosnan reconsider. So, no doubt, did the lack of attention given Brosnan's feature Nomads, a quick fizzle released last March. Finally, he said, "I thought, if I don't do Bond and some other guy gets it and I've been such a strong contender, I'm going to be really p***** off."

'Brosnan had begun to feel almost as if fate had assigned him the role. Bond, he said, was "part of my upbringing." Among the first films he saw when he moved from Ireland to England in the early '60s were Bond flicks. "For an Irish boy, age of 11, really green, very naive, sheltered Catholic upbringing, it was just mindblowing." Some 20 years later, he would meet the maker of those movies face-to-face. It was 1981, and Brosnan's miniseries, The Manions of America, was set to premiere in America. He and wife Cassie had had to borrow $3,500 to pay for their trip to L.A., but soon he was cast as Remington Steele (after Anthony Andrews turned down the role).

'Cassie, it so happened, was playing one of Bond's girls in the 1981 flick For Your Eyes Only--and they were invited to dinner at Broccoli's estate. "I remember turning to Cassie that night in this old Rent-a-Wreck car, and I was joking the whole way home saying, 'My name's Bond, James Bond.' I said, 'This is it, darling, there's no looking back now'--little knowing that five years on, one would be stepping into the role. There are a lot of funny things that happen in one's life." So there are. A few weeks ago, Brosnan returned to L.A., and there, barring strikes or other acts of a merciful God, he will begin shooting Remington Steele next October...'

Now that a furious Pierce Brosnan was out of the picture, Cubby Broccoli (apparently on the advice of his wife Dana) turned to Timothy Dalton and offered him the part of James Bond in The Living Daylights. Broccoli had always liked Dalton and always kept note of his career. Broccoli described Dalton as - "A vanishing breed, a gentleman actor with a highly tolerable ego!" However Dalton, who was now 40 years-old, declined the part because of existing theatrical commitments (in 1986, Dalton appeared in both Antony and Cleopatra and The Taming of the Shrew). Dalton's schedule was also complicated by a Brooke Shields adventure film called Brenda Starr he had signed up to appear in.

This then was the third time that Dalton had been approached about playing Bond and the third time he had recoiled from the overtures. This time was slightly different though in that Dalton's hands were tied (this was also the first time too that he had actually been offered the part). Dalton was contracted to both a play and a movie so was simply unavailable. It was tough luck but Dalton, who was never really that interested in stardom, wasn't unduly bothered by having to turn down James Bond, certainly in comparison to Brosnan - who was crestfallen to lose the part of Bond at the last minute.

With both Pierce Brosnan and Timothy Dalton apparently out of the running, this opened the door for any number of other actors to come into contention to play James Bond in The Living Daylights. It was rather like a tennis tournament where the top two seeds have been knocked out early and so everyone now fancies their chances! The New Zealand actor Sam Neill was now the preferred choice of many at EON to become the new Bond. The television series Reilly, Ace Of Spies and a suave turn as the diabolical Damien Thorn in the trashy Omen III had made Neill a viable 007 candidate. It was arranged for him to do a screen test (as ever with Bond auditions he acted out a From Russia with Love scene) at Pinewood but Neill was atrocious in the audition and seemed disinterested. Cubby Broccoli was never really sold on Sam Neill and the dire screentest merely confirmed his opinion.

Years later, Sam Neill explained his low energy Bond audition when he said he had no interest at all in playing James Bond and had been pressured into the audition by his agent. "I don't know why I was asked to audition, but I was, and I did, against my better judgment. My agent, who has now left this mortal coil, so I suppose I can say what I like. But she was deluded about certain things, and one of her delusions was that Bond would've been good for me, and vice versa, so I went very reluctantly out to test for that. And to my great relief, I didn't get the part, and I haven't looked back. It was one of the worst days of my life. I didn't want to be there, and I was so uncomfortable all day. There was nothing good about the day at all."

Another actor who auditioned to be James Bond in 1986 was Mark Greenstreet. Greenstreet had just appeared in a miniseries called Brat Farrar and spent three days doing screen tests at Pinewood. Greenstreet later said that during a break he went to use the toilet and bumped into Michael Biehn in his Corporal Hicks colonial space marine costume (James Cameron was shooting Aliens at the studio while Greenstreet's auditions took place). The interesting thing about Greenstreet is that he was only 25 at the time - which suggests EON, at some point, had a vague idea about making Bond much younger than usual.

Greenstreet spoke about his James Bond test in an appearance on Terry Wogan's chat show. Greenstreet said the first scene didn't go terribly well because he trapped his finger in a door while trying to make a suave entrance! Terry Wogan also commented on Greenstreet's hair and said it would be very strange to have a blond Bond! Michael Praed, the star of the TV show Robin Sherwood, was another actor who tested for The Living Daylights. Praed did his Bond audition with Fiona Fullerton. Marcus Gilbert was another young actor seemingly in contention. Gilbert was a dashing actor with male model good looks who had appeared in The Masks of Death (starring Peter Cushing as Sherlock Holmes) and Biggles: Adventures in Time. Gilbert would become best known for the television miniseries Riders.

The French actor Lambert Wilson (who spoke perfect English) was also a candidate. He was in his late twenties and had acted with Sean Connery in the 1982 film Five Days One Summer. Wilson screen tested for The Living Daylights opposite Maryam d'Abo as Tatiana Romanova, re-enacting scenes from

From Russia with Love. In his memoir, Cubby Broccoli said he liked Lambert Wilson and would have happily hired him but he said Michael G. Wilson wasn't convinced. The director John Glen was quite keen on Highlander star Christophe Lambert playing Bond in The Living Daylights but Lambert's heavily accented and not exactly fluent English made this an unlikely prospect. The search for Bond in The Living Daylights became so labyrinthe in the end that even American soap stars like John James and Michael Nader were said to be under consideration.

Bond fans used to wonder if Finlay Light was even real. A newspaper article in 1986 claimed he was a 32 year-old Australian model who had signed a ten year contract to become the new Bond but any evidence of Finlay Light being a real person was thin on the ground. However, while he didn't get the part he was actually real. John Glen confirmed in his memoir that Finlay Light tested for The Living Daylights. The Australian actor Andrew Clarke (who looked a lot like Tom Selleck and even had a tache) was another Australian candidate to play James Bond in The Living Daylights. In his memoir, John Glen said that Clarke was a 'front runner' for quite some time. Clarke played Simon Templar in a 1987 TV film pilot.

MGM's new chief Jerry Weintraub suggested they should break the bank and cast Mel Gibson as Bond. Gibson would later say that he turned down James Bond twice because the part didn't interest him. Tom Mankiewicz, writer on Bond films for Cubby Brocoli, disputed this though and said it was Cubby Broccoli who didn't want Gibson and not the other way around. According to Mankiewicz, Cubby felt Gibson was too famous and they would end up making a Mel Gibson movie rather than a James Bond movie. Cubby is also alleged to have felt that the 5'9 Gibson was far too short to play James Bond. "Cubby had a thing about tall people," said Mankiewicz. "Bond had to be tall, and Mel Gibson was too short."

Another Australian candidate was 35 year-old Anthony

Hamilton - a dancer, model and actor. He took over the main role in the series Cover Up after the death of the series' lead actor Jon-Erik Hexum and had a small part in Jumpin' Jack Flash with Whoopi Goldberg. Hamilton was tested by EON and felt to be a good candidate. It is alleged that Hamilton's sexuality though may have harmed his chances of playing the part. Barbara Broccoli is also said to have courted yet another Australian for the role in the shape of Bryan Brown. Brown was said to have no interest in being tied down to a long term contract though so this made any attempt to audition him pointless. Another potential candidate was Biggles star Neil Dickson though it's hard to see how the diminutive Dickson would have got past Cubby's obsessive height stipulations!

At some point during the casting process, Timothy Dalton became available again when his theatrical schedule unexpectedly cleared. Cubby Broccoli, who was clearly not convinced by any of the other candidates, decided to approach Dalton again and offer him the part of Bond in the Living Daylights. Cubby offered to push the production of The Living Daylights back by six weeks so that Timothy could fufil his obligation to appear in the film Brenda Starr. This was now the FOURTH time that EON had spoken to Dalton about becoming Bond - stretching right back to the late 1960s. Surprisingly though, Dalton was still not completely convinced he should take the role. Time was running out at this point so Broccoli continued to test actors - some it seems as a deliberate ploy to persuade Dalton.

Robert Bathurst, later best known for the television show Cold Feet, claims he tested to play Bond for The Living Daylights but thought it was only to put pressure on Timothy Dalton to make a decision. Bathurst was about 30 at the time and had mostly appeared in comedy shows. "Oh, that was such a ludicrous audition," said Bathurst. "I could never have done it - Bond actors are always very different to me. But some casting director persuaded me to go. The thing was, they already had Timothy Dalton. But I think he hadn't signed yet so they wanted to tell him, 'They're still seeing people, you know,' to put pressure on him to sign. I was just an arm-twisting exercise.

Cubby Broccoli's persistence finally paid off and Timothy Dalton signed on to become the fourth official James Bond actor. Dalton later said he was at an airport when he decided to accept the Bond offer. "I'd taken the Concorde from London to Miami to catch and make a connection to go up to Jacksonville to start Brenda Starr... and the Concorde was late! Or something went wrong, anyway, and I was stuck in the Miami airport. There was a hotel there in the airport, and I took a room there. Without anything to do, I decided to start thinking about whether I really, really should or should not do James Bond. Although obviously we'd moved some way along in that process, I just wasn't set on whether I should do it or shan't I do it. But the moment of truth was fast approaching as to whether I'd say yes or no. And that's where I said yes. I picked up the phone from the hotel room in the Miami airport and called them and said, "Yep, you're on: I'll do it.""

Interestingly, EON insisted that Timothy Dalton do a screen test before he could be officially signed as Bond. Dalton was reluctant to do this and felt that his body of work was more than sufficient evidence for them to judge him. "Look, nobody doubts your talents," Michael G. Wilson told Dalton, "but we have to see you as Bond, just to get an idea of what we're dealing with, what we have on camera." Dalton eventually agreed to the test and it all went fine. He scrubbed as well as you might expect and looked preposterously handsome in his test. EON felt like they had made the right choice and were confident that Timothy Dalton was going to be a terrific Bond.

Dalton was at 6'2 the tallest actor to be cast in the part. After the tongue-in-cheek nature of the Roger Moore era, the casting of Dalton was a bold decision by Cubby Broccoli. It automatically guaranteed that the next film would be a less flippant and jovial affair than Roger's movies had been. But would audiences miss the fun and humour? Only time would tell. "I couldn't see myself taking over and not doing it my own way," said Dalton, "to try and capture Fleming's Bond. He's tarnished. He's not a superclean hero. He's not a white knight. He drinks, smokes. He suffers from this thing called accidie, a moral malaise or confusion which makes him... thoroughly like us."

Given that, to this day, Bond fans sometimes wonder what Goldeneye would be like with Timothy Dalton (as we shall see later in the book, this is something which could have happened), it only seems reasonable to wonder too what The Living Daylights might have been like with Pierce Brosnan. On the evidence of Brosnan's performance in the 1987 film The Fourth Protocol (and of course Goldeneye eight years later), Brosnan would have been perfectly fine in The Living Daylights. Brosnan probably would have made the film somewhat lighter with his presence (Dalton simply had more depth and subtext to his acting than Brosnan) but Brosnan would clearly have been more at home with the Bond quips than Dalton.

You can easily imagine Brosnan in most of The Living Daylights. He'd have been terrific in the Aston Martin ice chase sequence and would have made a competent fist of the more dramatic moments in the story. Brosnan later said he was relieved that he didn't get Daylights because in retrospect he was too young and felt more appropriately mature and confident in 1994 when he did get the part. I'm not sure I agree with this though. If you watch Brosnan in The Fourth Protocol (which was made around the same time as Daylights) it's easy to picture the Brosnan of that era making a very good Bond.

EON haven't cast a really young actor as Bond since George Lazenby. Even Daniel Craig (who was supposed to be a young Bond new to the service in Casino Royale) was a rather mature looking 38 year-old when he got the part. Casting a 33 year-old Pierce Brosnan in Daylights would have been quite radical in hindsight - especially as Bond was played by a 57 year-old actor in the previous film. It would certainly be interesting to see EON go down the Lazenby path again in the future one day and cast a really young actor. Brosnan in 1986 is the closest they have ever got to doing this though at the time of writing.

One advantage Timothy Dalton had over Brosnan is that his Bond was more enigmatic. Dalton's Bond was more of a quiet thinker. Brosnan was more of a tabula rasa in comparison. Not to say Brosnan wasn't good. Most people feel Brosnan was much better than the scripts he got in his Bond films. The essential difference between the two interpretations is that Brosnan's Bond seemed to mostly be having a good time. He seemed to enjoy being a secret agent. Dalton's Bond did not have this quality. Dalton's Bond was more like Fleming's Bond in that he often questioned the harsh realities of his profession.

CHAPTER FOUR

The director on The Living Daylights was John Glen - here returning to helm his fourth Bond film in a row. Glen directed all the eighties Bond films (For Your Eyes Only, Octopussy, A View To A Kill, The Living Daylights, and Licence to Kill) and first began his long association with the series when he worked as an editor and second unit director on Peter Hunt's On Her Majesty's Secret Service in the late 1960s. Glen still remains somewhat unappreciated by James Bond fans these days despite directing more 007 films than anyone else. Glen was very good with action sequences in particular. There was no serious thought to replacing John Glen on Daylights. Cubby presumably felt that as they had a new Bond actor it would be best to keep the familiar nuts and bolts of the franchise in place around him.

Cubby Broccoli tended to rely on a fairly small circle of British directors that he knew and trusted. Terence Young, Guy Hamilton, and Lewis Gilbert all made more than one Bond film - though Peter Hunt, who was an editor on the Bond series, only directed On Her Majesty's Secret Service. One could argue that Cubby was quite conservative when it came to selecting directors. He tended to favour experienced directors that he personally knew well. Handing the director's chair to John Glen in 1981 was probably the boldest thing Cubby did but by then Glen was something of a Bond veteran anyway. John Glen had more or less been groomed for this promotion. Cubby's preference for choosing people he knew was hardly a negative though as all of the directors he used directed some terrific Bond pictures between them.

John Glen was born in Sunbury-on-Thames in 1932 and remembers growing up during the war and the early years in the British film industry. Glen always seemed genuinely enthusiastic about Bond and grateful for having been given the opportunity to work on the series. On Her Majesty's Secret Service was the 'Alpine' Bond with extensive ski sequences and

Glen's second unit duties on this spectacular film were excellent. Perhaps his finest hour though in this capacity was the pre title sequence of The Spy Who Loved Me where Bond skis off a mountain range into infinity before his Union Jack parachute opens. It was Glen who hiked up a mountain in Baffin Island with his film unit to capture this legendary stunt.

After second unit and editing duties on three previous Bonds, Glen said it was a great honour when he was 'promoted' by Broccoli and allowed to direct a James Bond film himself with For Your Eyes Only. Glen says that he tried to make the Bond films more grounded when he took over and one can say he did this with For Your Eyes Only and the two Timothy Dalton films he helmed. Glen's Octopussy and A View To A Kill, while great fun at times, are rather daft though it has to be said! John Glen's approach to Bond was that it had to be cheeky and audacious, larger than life. Panache was important. While the relationship between Dalton and Glen, as we shall see later, was occasionally tense, there is no doubt that John Glen enjoyed the challenge of introducing a new Bond actor and clearly upped his game for The Living Daylights.

Mathilda May (forever immortal as the nude space vampire from Tobe Hooper's Lifeforce) unsuccessfully auditioned for the part of love interest Kara Milovy in The Living Daylights. The Australian model and actress Virginia Hey (who had appeared in Mad Max 2 and the Aussie soap Neighbours, among other credits) also read for the part of Kara. Hey was unsuccessful but was given a small part as Rubavitch in The Living Daylights. Maryam d'Abo, who was a former model, was eventually cast as Kara.

Maryam d'Abo had (luckily as it turned out) bumped into Barbara Broccoli after getting a short haircut and Broccoli felt that d'Abo might have the right mix of vulnerability and beauty neccessary for Kara. In 1984, d'Abo had unsuccessfully auditioned for the role of Pola Ivanova in A View to a Kill. Maryam d'Abo was actually cast in Daylights when Pierce Brosnan was going to play Bond so she saw her leading man change before the cameras had even rolled!

Times were very different when The Living Daylights went into production. Whereas Sean Connery and Roger Moore had often clocked up their first conquest by the time the pre-credit sequence had ended, Timothy Dalton had (if one discounts the woman on the yacht in the PTS!) just Maryam d'Abo for company in The Living Daylights. In an era of AIDS, the relationship between them was often more romantic rather than suggestive - at least by the standards of a James Bond film. The romance between Bond and Kara was more believable and realistic compared to many other Bond films.

Richard Maibaum called Timothy Dalton the best actor to play James Bond and said he was looking forward to a more grounded sort of Bond film. If a 1983 interview he conducted with Starlog for the release of Octopussy is anything to go by, Richard Maibaum hadn't been the biggest fan of Roger Moore's Bond. Maibaum felt the films had become too tongue-in-cheek and complained that Roger kept changing lines in script in favour of his own quips! Maibaum's general thesis was that Bond needed to get back to the wonderful Sean Connery era - where the leading man felt more dangerous.

While this was true enough (and Dalton wanted Bond to feel more dangerous too), Richard Maibaum seemed to rather overstate how down to earth or grounded the Connery films had been. The Connery era had as many quips and gadgets as the Roger Moore films and Connery's Bond was fairly indestructible and unflappable most of the time. The one time you really genuinely feared for Connery's Bond was during his encounter on the train with Robert Shaw's Red Grant in From Russia with Love. That was a wonderfully tense encounter and one of the greatest sequences in Bond history.

"He has a wonderful voice because of his Shakespearean training," said John Glen of Timothy Dalton. "He's going to make this part his own, and initially that may shock people. When Tim is holding a gun, he truly looks like a man with a licence to kill." Glen said that Dalton had a jaded world-weariness about him which would make him a departure from Sean Connery and Roger Moore. As for Bond being a sexist dinosaur, Glen said - "I think Bond is a great lover of women. He respects women, but he uses women, as I think happens in real life. But he also has a softer side to his nature, as you'll see in his relationship with Maryam d'Abo."

Now that Roger Moore had been replaced by an actor nearly twenty years his junior, a new Moneypenny was required for The Living Daylights. Replacing the legendary Lois Maxwell (who had played Moneypenny in the Connery, Lazenby, and Moore films) was Caroline Bliss. Bliss had only a few TV credits to her name and had once played Princess Diana. Rather like Timothy Dalton, her first love was the stage. Bliss auditioned for Moneypenny and was later told she had the part by her agent in the theatre bar one night after she had come off the stage. She was taken to Pinewood to meet Timothy Dalton just to make sure they had some chemistry together. Fortunately, Dalton and Bliss found they had some mutual friends in common so they found it very easy to talk and get along.

Caroline Bliss was still only in her twenties when she made The Living Daylights and remains the only actress to play the part in spectacles. In a strange quirk of fate, Caroline Bliss was a childhood friend of Samantha Bond - who replaced her as Moneypenny for the Pierce Brosnan films in the 1990s. Bliss said it was amazing to step onto the set of a Bond film for the first time. Her only apprehension was that she would be replacing a legend in Lois Maxwell. Bliss later said that although she wouldn't have turned the role down for the world, becoming part of the James Bond franchise did overshadow her career and that she didn't find the part of Moneypenny especially fulfilling because it was such a small role. Bliss only spent a few days at Pinewood shooting her Moneypenny scenes.

The imposing Julie T Wallace, who plays Rosika Miklos

(Bond's Bratislava contact at the TransSiberian Pipeline), came to the attention of the Bond producers with her fine breakthrough performance on British television the previous year as Ruth in the cult miniseries The Life and Loves of a She-Devil. She appeared in another Timothy Dalton film, the interesting although little seen 'Hawks', the year after The Living Daylights came out. The German dancer and actor Andreas Wisniewski is also well cast as the deadly henchman Necros. A-Ha's (the theme song artists for Daylights) lead singer Morten Harket was offered a small role as a villain's henchman (possibly Necros?) in the film but he declined this invitation.

An excellent supporting cast was assembled for The Living Daylights. Jeroen Krabbé and Joe Don Baker were respectively cast as the baddies General Georgi Koskov and Brad Whitaker. The ever dependable Art Malik, John Rhys-Davies, and Thomas Wheatley took on supporting roles, and John Terry became the latest actor to play Felix Leiter. The Living Daylights would mark the first appearance by Felix Leiter since David Hedison portrayed the character in Live and Let Die in 1973. Series regulars Desmond Llewelyn, Robert Brown, Geoffrey Keen, and Walter Gotell would all return respectively as Q, M, Minister of Defence, and General Anatol Gogol. Apart from Moneypenny, there was no shake-up at all when it came to the Universal Exports team.

There were plans for a big bazaar sequence in The Living Daylights but this didn't get shot in the end. This idea seems to have been later recycled and used in the PTS of Tomorrow Never Dies a decade later. At one point, Charles and Diana (obviously played by actors) were going to have a cameo at the end of The Living Daylights in the same fashion that Margaret and Dennis Thatcher featured at the end of For Your Eyes Only. Thankfully though this plan was axed and abandoned before it got very far (apparently an actor had been cast as Prince Charles before the plug was sensibly pulled on this idea).

The Aston Martin has been an iconic part of the Bond series since Goldfinger. Sean Connery disliked the car because he found it small and uncomfortable but there was no doubt the Aston Martin looked terrific onscreen - especially equipped with Bond style gadgets. Roger Moore never actually drove an Aston Martin in his Bond films (although, curiously, he DID drive one in the 1981 comedy film The Cannonball Run). It was decided when Roger Moore became Bond not to immediately saddle him with too many of the iconic 007 trappings associated with Sean Connery. It took three films, for example, before we saw Roger in a naval commander uniform. The initial reluctance to invite comparisons between Moore and Connery was shrewd and helped Roger Moore to make the part his own. Roger Moore's Bond was associated with the Lotus but never the Aston Martin.

The Aston Martin returned for The Living Daylights and has been a regular part of the series ever since. We saw Pierce Brosnan drive an Aston Martin and Daniel Craig too. The Daniel Craig era though has seen you might describe as an over reliance on the Aston Martin - to the point where the car has arguably lost some of its novelty and become almost too familiar. Sam Mendes would wheel the Aston Martin out with a great fanfare in his Bond films as if he expected the audience to stand up and wildly applaud at the sight of a car they'd already seen dozens of times! You could actually make a case for the Aston Martin having a rest in the Bond franchise and the next Bond actor driving a different car for a change. Still, there few things as associated with James Bond as the Aston Martin and in The Living Daylights it was a novelty to see the car in action again.

The Living Daylights had a budget of $40 million. In today's money that would be like having over $90 million to make a film. The film was shot at Pinewood Studios at its 007 Stage in the United Kingdom, as well as Weissensee in Austria. Other locations included Germany, Gibraltar, the United States, and Italy, while the desert scenes were shot in Ouarzazate, Morocco. The Prince and Princess of Wales visited the production of the film at Pinewood and Diana famously got to smash a prop bottle over Charles' head. This was probably something she felt like doing in real life in years to come!

Timothy Dalton flew into London on September the 29th 1986 to begin work on The Living Daylights. Only the previous day he had finished his stint on the Brooke Shields film Brenda Starr in Florida (he needn't have bothered as Brenda Starr sat on the shelf for two years and bombed when it was released) and with no rehearsal time was now immediately plunged into by far the biggest role of his career. The delay caused by Brosnan leaving the role had given allowed Dalton the extra time necessary to finish Brenda Starr and make a decision about Bond. Although Dalton was something of a reluctant Bond he impressed everyone with his dedication once ensconced in the role.

Dalton read all the Fleming novels in preparation and was arguably the most intelligent of the men who have played Bond. Dalton would give interviews where he talked about things like Harold Pinter and "accidie" - Fleming's definition of boredom and the deadliest of all sins for James Bond. Ever hear Daniel Craig or George Lazenby talking about Pinter's distilled essence of naturalism and how art is not reality but the appearance of whatever reality is appropriate? In an age before CGI, Dalton also threw himself into the stuntwork and performed many of 007's death defying feats. That jeep careening down the Rock of Gibraltar? That's really Timothy Dalton strapped to the top.

When asked about doing stunts in the film though, Dalton was rather coy and modest. "This is the sort of question that you should not be asking," he said. "Cinema is magic. When people pay their money and go sit inside a cinema, they must believe. And programs like this, I mean, betray all our tricks. You wouldn't expect a conjurer or a magician to give his tricks away. Now the truth of the matter is that audiences are very sophisticated now and there's been too many questions like this asked of very many films, and we know there're stuntmen and we've got a terrific team of stuntmen on this movie. Very, very highly skilled professionals led by Paul Weston. Stuntmen do stunts, and I do as much action as I can. But you must believe it's me. If you believe it's me, it's me. Otherwise and audience would feel betrayed."

In a set visit interview by Prevue Magazine, Dalton said (perhaps rather tongue-in-cheek) of his new role - "I suppose after a while the part will become rote, but, with big budgets, tight scripts, good actors to work with and the weight of the films resting on my shoulders, I know I'll never take the character for granted. I'm trying to bring something new to the role, so that neither the audience nor can I get bored; I'm attempting to inject something different - an expression, some humor, and interesting nuance - into every take, into every scene. Perhaps the 007 image will get a tad more intellectual. Who knows? They may tag me the thinking man's James Bond." Timothy Dalton was at pains to distance James Bond from contemporary action movie rivals like Rambo and Schwarzenegger. Dalton said that James Bond used ingenuity rather than brawn and wouldn't be seen dead pumping iron in a gym.

Despite the media interest in the new James Bond actor, the press found Timothy Dalton a difficult person to write about because his private life was a complete mystery. Dalton had no interest at all in being a celebrity and was notoriously protective of his privacy. He rarely spoke about anything except acting. The press found it difficult to get much of an impression on Dalton as a person because he was basically invisible unless obliged to promote a film. "I live a pretty quiet lifestyle when I am not working," Dalton told Playgirl on the Daylights set at Pinewood. "I don't generally get too involved in the social whirl and the party scene, it doesn't really interest me very much. And when I'm working I don't have any time to get into trouble anyway. After a full day of this sort of stuff, you have absolutely no difficulty falling asleep at night, believe me!"

Timothy Dalton shot an alternative gunbarrel opening for The Living Daylights in which he does a little jump as he turns around to fire at the screen. You can find this unused gunbarrel on YouTube quite easily and you can see why it wasn't used. It does look a bit silly! The only previous James Bond gunbarrel that tried to do something different was when George Lazenby dropped to his knee before shooting at the screen. That idea sort of worked (although Peter Hunt apparently never cared for it much) but Dalton doing a little jump in his gunbarrel plainly didn't work and so it was wisely dropped.

If Dalton had any fears that becoming James Bond might hinder his stage career, these were soon happily quashed. Dalton said that becoming James Bond had been no hindrance to his stage career at all. If anything it had actually given his theatrical career a nice boost. "Last year I did a play in the West End of London," said Dalton, "a Eugene O'Neill play, called A Touch of the Poet with Vanessa (Redgrave). In fact you interviewed her when we were doing The Taming of the Shrew together. We always got people at the stage door who came and said, 'I've never been to the theater before. I only came because you were James Bond.' They didn't expect to see this little gray-haired, paunchy drunkard on the stage. And said they loved it and they were going to come to the theater again, so it helps to fill the theater, it brings people, it's no hindrance whatsoever."

There was no official press conference to unveil Timothy Dalton as Bond. This was a contrast to Pierce Brosnan in 1994 and Daniel Craig in 2005. These days you simply can't imagine them casting a new James Bond actor without arranging a fancy press conference to unveil him. Bond fans (and the media) would feel cheated if this didn't happen. Dalton simply went straight into shooting the film. The press only got to meet Timothy Dalton when a press conference was held during the Daylights shoot in Vienna on October the 5th 1986. Timothy Dalton and Maryam d'Abo also posed for photographers with an Aston Martin V8 Volante. Dalton wore a light blue suit (which doesn't feature in the film) and looked fantastic.

Cubby Broccoli got slightly irritated during the press conference when he was asked if James Bond was still relevant. Cubby told the press that The Living Daylights would be a much more serious film than they were used to and would hark back to the Fleming novels. Timothy Dalton was happy to concur with this mission statement. "Roger can climb out of a pocket aeroplane and give a glib remark, I can't," said Dalton in one of his later Daylights interviews. There was no point hiring Timothy Dalton if you were planning to make Octopussy or Moonraker. For better or for worse, things were now going to change.

If his later comments are anything to go by though, Timothy Dalton felt there was still some resistance to trying to make a much more down to earth James Bond film at the time. He wasn't quite sure that EON and the studio were completely on the same page as him. "The prevailing wisdom at the time—which I would say I shared—was that the series, whilst very entertaining, had become rather spoof-like," said Dalton in 2014. "It was one-liners and raised eyebrows and it had become, let's say, too lighthearted. And the producer, Mr. Broccoli, felt that, and he wanted to try and bring it back to something more like its original roots with those Sean Connery films. I had loved them all, and I had loved the books.

"But I think ultimately for anything to be successful, an audience must empathise. They must also get involved, but they must be given enough to suspend disbelief so that they're truly able to become involved with the story. That's not to say that there can't be any comedy. There should always be comedy. Comedy is a great thing. So that was the loose framework that we sort of embarked on, but then you find that nobody else wants to change it all! The studio doesn't want to change it, the people that work on it don't want to change it. Everyone's happy with what they know. And everyone intellectually says, "Well, yes, we should, it was getting a bit stale, it was getting a bit this, that, and the other," but nobody actually wants to. So it wasn't as easy as one would hope."

Dalton cut the size of Bond's wardrobe by about a third in comparison to the previous 007 films. He had firm ideas about what Bond should or shouldn't wear and how his lifestyle should be depicted. "Bond was never flash or ostentatious," said Dalton of the books. "In fact, he really wore a uniform, a dark suit, navy blue. He was very navy blue. He wasn't a wealthy man. He used his money to buy the best that he needed, but then he kept it. For example, his suitcase. At one time it was a very good suitcase. But he's had it for ten years."

Timothy Dalton impressed everyone during the shoot with his complete lack of ego. He was unfailingly polite and down to earth and there was no diva behaviour at all. Dalton also got on well with co-star Maryam d'Abo and one can therefore see a genuine affection in their onscreen chemistry. Making a Bond film can be a rather tough assignment for the lead actor because they are in nearly every scene and a Bond shoot takes about six months. When you factor in the physical exertions of stunts (Dalton was obviously more involved in this side of Bond than Roger Moore had been!), then you can see how The Living Daylights was no picnic for Timothy Dalton. Dalton said he hardly got any days off on Daylights and struggled to stay awake during some of the night shoots. He was exhausted by the end.

More than anything it was Dalton's intensity that impressed the crew after years of jovial Roger Moore extravaganzas. "You really believed he was going to kill him," said director of photography Alec Mills on a scene where Dalton's Bond has to tangle with a villain. The Living Daylights was the last film that Cubby Broccoli produced hands-on before his age and failing health caught up with him. Dalton's era also marked the last contributions of the great composer John Barry, screenwriter Richard Maibaum, titles designer Maurice Binder, actor Robert Brown as M, and in-house director John Glen to the series. The Living Daylights was also notably the last true Cold War James Bond film produced. In many ways the two Dalton films were the end of an era.

CHAPTER FIVE

The PTS of The Living Daylights features an exciting and entertaining sequence in which the Double O section agents attempt to penetrate the radar installations of Gibraltar in a training exercise. SAS soldiers based on the colony are assigned to stop them. With their faces covered (so we don't who the new 007 is among them) the men jump out of a Hercules transport plane above the Rock. 002 lands in a tree and is captured while two other OO agents begin to scale the cliffs towards the base. It is sometimes said the OO agents in the PTS are made to look like previous Bond actors but I've never noticed much obvious similarity myself! Is the foppish blond haired 002 supposed to be Roger Moore? He doesn't look like him much.

An assassin appears and sends a tag reading Smert' Shpionam (Death to Spies) down the rope to 004 before cutting it and killing him. We cut to 007 as the screams ring out.

Timothy Dalton is given a simple, effective, and excellent introduction in his first shot as James Bond. Dalton's Bond is introduced as a dashing man of action. Bond takes off after the mysterious assassin and jumps onto his Land Rover, clinging on as it races through narrow roads and eventually goes over the edge of a tourist spot towards the sea. Bond escapes with his reserve parachute while the assassin is killed when the Land Rover explodes in mid-air. Timothy Dalton's willingness to be in the thick of the stunt-work whenever possible reaps its reward all through the sequence.

Maurice Binder's title sequence is rather uninspired although A-Ha's theme song (of which more later) is not bad at all. The Pet Shop Boys were originally hired to write the theme song for The Living Daylights. Their instrumental demo for the theme, which you can easily find on YouTube, was rejected and the job went to A-Ha in the end (much to the annoyance of John Barry you suspect). The Pet Shop Boys demo is catchy and interesting if nothing else and had some potential for John Barry to sprinkle it with his Bond stardust. The Pet Shop Boys later reworked their rejected Bond theme into This Must Be The Place I Waited Years To Leave.

Fleming's original short story is faithfully adhered to in the early part of the movie. 007 helps KGB General Koskov (Jeroen Krabbé) defect to the West. As he guards his escape with a sniper rifle, 007 sees that the sniper protecting Koskov is the cellist Kara Milovy from the concert hall in Bratislava. He refuses to kill her and shoots the rifle out of her hands whilst ensuring Koskov's escape from the hall. In a safe-house in England, General Koskov informs MI6 that the KGB is being run by power-hungry General Leonid Pushkin (an enjoyable John Rhys-Davies).

According to Koskov, Pushkin has revived an old policy of Smert' Shpionam and needs to be eliminated. A group led by the assassin Necros (Andreas Wisniewski) raids the country-house (where the British Secret Service have Koskov) and snatch him back. Necros disguises himself as a milkman (complete with explosive milk bottles!) to gain entry and his kitchen fight with a member of security is splendid stuff and very brutal for a James Bond film. Necros also has his own theme tune - 'Where Has Every Body Gone?' by The Pretenders. How very apt!

Bond is sent to kill General Pushkin. In an enjoyable Q scene, 007 is given an electric key-finder featuring skeleton keys and capable of exploding and releasing stun-gas (the explosive is triggered by a wolf whistle) and an Aston Martin. Bond uses the Aston Martin to great effect later on with rockets and a laser built into the wheel in the ice-chase as they escape to Austria. Prior to this 007 returns to Bratislava. Suspecting that Koskov is not all that he seems he poses as his friend to gain Kara's trust. The scenes in Kara's apartment are very low-key and surprisingly human and dramatic for a Bond film.

At the opera in Vienna, Bond excuses himself from Milovy to

meet his MI6 contact, Saunders, in a fairground café. Saunders has investigated Koskov's story and discovered a link between him and a greedy arms dealer "General" Brad Whitaker (Joe Don Baker). The Stradivarius Kara owns, though bought by Koskov, was paid for by Brad Whitaker. Whitaker had arranged to supply the KGB with Western high-technology weapons through Koskov, and Koskov is attempting to deliver the down payment in diamonds. Pushkin is in fact investigating Koskov, and Koskov wanted the British to kill him.

As Saunders leaves the café he is killed by Necros, who detonates a bomb by slamming the sliding front door of the café on Saunders. Thomas Wheatley has a small but memorable part as Saunders and we do feel for him as he heads to his death. Necros leaves behind a balloon with the words Smert' Shpionam on it, unaware that Bond already suspects the true motives behind the trail of clues left for him. Bond returns to Kara and they immediately leave for Tangier and Morocco, where Whitaker operates.

007 and Pushkin meet. Pushkin reveals to Bond that he had been investigating Koskov for embezzlement of government funds, and adds that the KGB scrapped Smert' Shpionam decades earlier, confirming Bond's suspicions that a third party is behind the plot. 007 fakes Pushkin's death at a convention in Tangier by 'shooting' him just before Necros. He escapes over the rooftops and is eventually picked up by John Terry's Felix Leiter. Terry is given a very thankless task in his tiny scene and doesn't make for a memorable Leiter.

The rooftop chase was supposed to escalate into the magic-carpet scene and a motorbike chase. If you've seen the Ultimate Edition DVD of The Living Daylights where these deleted scenes are available, you'll know why they cut them. They simply didn't suit the tone of the film or Timothy Dalton's 007. Koskov persuades Kara that 007 is a KGB agent intent on killing her. She drugs him with a Martini but it is too late when 007 convinces her that she has been tricked by

Koskov. They are flown to a Soviet Base in Afghanistan but escape with the aid of Kamran Shah (Art Malik), a Mujahideen fighter. It is obviously somewhat awkward today that the Afghan freedom fighters in the film are the people who became the Taliban! A year later, Rambo III did the same thing and made Afghan freedom fighters the heroes.

Bond discovers that Whitaker and Koskov are paying diamonds for a large shipment of opium for distribution in the US and funds for Soviet arms. The Mujahideen help Bond and Milovy infiltrate the air base. Bond plants a bomb in the back of the cargo aeroplane transporting the drugs, but Koskov spots him. Bond takes the aeroplane as the Mujahideen attack the airbase. Kara makes it onto the plane at the last minute but so does Necros who attacks 007 as he tries to defuse a bomb. An exciting fight follows as the cargo doors open and they fall out clinging onto the cargo net. 007 gains the upper hand and cuts Necros' bootlaces to send him to his death. He defuses the bomb and drops it over a bridge to help the Mujahideen who are in retreat from the Soviets.

007 travels to Whitaker's house and interrupts a game of toy soldiers to tell him the opium is gone. Whitaker uses a high-tec machine-gun to try to kill Bond but Q's key-ring finder saves him in the end. "He met his Waterloo," says Bond. The KGB save Bond's life when Puskin's men burst in and kill the Whitaker guard about to shoot Bond. General Koskov is there, too, and, while not killed, he is to be flown back to Moscow "in the diplomatic bag". 007 heads back home and though assumed to be on assignment turns up in Kara's dressing-room in the closing scene of the film.

With lashings of intrigue, beautiful European locations, and a James Bond who nuts someone minutes into the film!, The Living Daylights was a refreshing change of gear after the excesses of the Roger Moore era. Timothy Dalton is closer to the Bond created by Ian Fleming than any of his predecessors. He is cold and aloof at times, we believe he can kill, but he is also very handsome and reasonably debonair so we also believe that he IS James Bond. His Bond is enigmatic and strikes one as a loner who is very professional, a man who carries a few psychological scars.

One can see why Cubby Broccoli always wanted Timothy Dalton to play Bond - although for Dalton and Dalton fans it probably ended up a case of too little too late. Dalton seems to take playing James Bond much more seriously than the previous actors. For this reason his contribution is debated to this day. Some feel that Dalton felt forced and humourless and others feel he nailed the part. As for humour, Timothy Dalton will never be able to deliver a line like "Amazing this modern safety glass..." like Roger Moore but he had a (sometimes truculent) charm that is mined to good effect in The Living Daylights. Stuffing Kara's cello onto the back seat of the Aston Martin and placing Koskov in the pipeline launch bay for example.

Timothy Dalton aside, what's great about The Living Daylights? Maryam d'Abo and her relationship with Bond is nicely developed. We do actually care about her and who wins her trust. John Barry's last James Bond score (which we'll discuss at the end of this chapter) is fantastic. His remix of the main theme for the Afghan battle is amazing and a reminder of how sorely missed he is. Though the film is much more down to earth than many in the series it still has enough Bond 'bumps' (Aston Martin chase with gadgets, John Barry, beautiful European locations, a Q scene, Moneypenny) to feel completely Bondian and cinematic and the photography for the Afghan scenes is quite superb.

Perhaps the plot is a trifle convoluted and the film does struggle to maintain momentum at times when the action switches to Afghanistan but it has several superb action sequences and Dalton's physical presence makes them all the more engaging. The Living Daylights is a good example of how to re position a long-running series like the Bond franchise without kicking up too much fuss. You could argue that Whitaker turns up too late in Daylights to be a truly effective villain. EON must have liked Joe Don Baker though because several years later they brought him back to the franchise as a completely different character in Goldeneye.

Jeroen Krabbé is an interesting villain in that he's more of a conman than anything. While he's entertaining one can understand criticisms that the two villains in the movie are a little vague and don't really earn a place in the illustrious hall of memorable Bond baddies. Caroline Bliss doesn't get much to do as Moneypenny but she's ok and seems to have the potential for good chemistry with Timothy Dalton. Sadly though we would never see Dalton and Bliss together again!

John Terry (who is a fine actor in other things) is rather wooden as Felix Leiter and has no chemistry at all with Timothy Dalton. It might have been better if they'd axed Leiter from the film altogether. Leiter would back in the next movie but John Terry would not. Generally, a few quibbles aside, the cast around Dalton is very good. It's Timothy Dalton who takes most of the plaudits though. Dalton's Bond in The Living Daylights might be the best Bond we've ever seen on the screen. He not only ticks the traditional Bondian casting checklist in that he's tall, dark, and handsome, but he's also brave enough to give us a weary Bond who is flawed and human.

The Living Daylights has some amazing action sequences and the fight between Necros and the agent at the safe house is one of the best punch ups we've ever seen in a Bond film. Although the film isn't perfect I would have Daylights comfortably inside my own James Bond top ten. When Bond drives away with Saunders and mutters "Stuff my orders! I only kill professionals. That girl didn't know one end of a rifle from the other. Go ahead, tell M what you want. If he fires me, I'll thank him for it. Whoever she was, it must've scared the living daylights out of her!" - well, that's one of the greatest pure Fleming's Bond moments we've ever had in the movie franchise.

The Living Daylights was greatly boosted by having the final 007 score of John Barry. The soundtrack album for Daylights is still worthy of your time. Norwegian pop group A-Ha were chosen to record the title song. By now, EON were in the business of trying to find modern and popular artists to record the themes to maximise commercial sales. This had began in 1985 when Duran Duran did the theme for A View To a Kill. It was the first time a modern pop band had got the 007 gig. This worked out very well though because Duran Duran's theme song was terrific and one of the best.

The main goal of EON since 1985 is to hire someone who is currently very popular and if they come up with a decent song then that's a bonus. Having the best prospective Bond theme song doesn't mean you will get chosen. The k.d. lang song Surrender for Tomorrow Never Dies is vastly superior (and much more Bondian) than Sheryl Crow's forgettable title theme but Surrender ended up on the end credits. Sheryl Crow was chosen because some studio bureaucrat obviously decided she was a bigger star and would sell more records. Forever - I Am All Yours by Eva Almér was a fantastic proposed theme song for Quantum of Solace but the truly atrocious Another Way to Die (surely the worst Bond theme of all time!) by Jack White and Alicia Keys was chosen instead.

A-Ha and John Barry did not get along very well working on the Daylights theme. It would be fair to say that they loathed one another. There were some creative differences over the theme and A-Ha later released their own version on one of their albums. However, Barry's version was vastly superior and thankfully that's the version we got in the movie. While the Daylights theme is not as good as the one by Duran Duran a few years earlier, it is perfectly fine for what it is and works surprisingly well with a Maurice Binder credit sequence. You wouldn't say A-Ha produced a classic Bond theme but it's solid enough and EON would serve up a lot worse when it comes to Bond themes in the decades to come.

The piece of music where Necros attacks the safe house has

some trademark John Barry brassiness and is rife with tension. The Pretenders' Where Has Everybody Gone is also used to nice effect in this sequence. The Daylights score is especially atmospheric and beautiful during the Bratislava sniper scenes. The music for the Aston Martin ice chase is a wonderfully Bondian mix of orchestra, drums, and bass with some fantastic horns. If one had a criticism of the Daylights score it might be the surfeit of flutes in some of the quieter scenes but Barry manages to avoid the score ever becoming cheesy or twee. The action cues when Koskov is sprung from the safe house are terrific and The Pretenders If There Was A Man makes a nice closing theme for the movie.

CHAPTER SIX

The Living Daylights had a $5.5 million marketing launch in the United States. In Britain, two books were released to coincide with the film - The James Bond Movie Book and The James Bond Movie Poster Book. A one hour documentary titled Happy Anniversary 007 was also televised. The poster for The Living Daylights was an excellent illustrated affair with Dalton in a tux surrounded by characters from the film. This was that era when posters were painted. Later Bond posters would be blighted by the new trend for movie posters to be bland collages. The tagline for the film was - 'The most dangerous Bond. Ever. Living on the edge. It's the only way he lives'. The Living Daylights had its World Premiere on the 29th of June 1987 at the Odeon Leicester Square, London.

Daylights received a fairly positive reception from critics with most of them feeling that Timothy Dalton was a welcome change of gear after thirteen years of Roger Moore. Dalton was praised by many critics for bringing the series back to earth and providing a more straight-laced interpretation of the character. Not everyone was won over though. Robert Ebert in particular seemed to think that Dalton was far too serious and lacked the charisma of Connery and the wit of Moore. A few other critics also complained that Dalton wasn't as good as Sean Connery - which felt like a rather unfair comparison. No one could ever be as good as Sean Connery was as Bond!

'Our Flick of the Week is one of the most eagerly awaited films of the summer,' wrote a hard to please Gene Siskel in the Chicago Tribune, 'the latest James Bond film, starring the fourth serious actor to play Bond, Timothy Dalton. He`s better than Roger Moore, who seemed to have disdain for the character and the audience. But Dalton simply doesn't have the manliness or the charm of Sean Connery. That`s not the only problem with the film, which tells the story of Bond trying to break up an international smuggling ring. The gadgets and gizmos, so much a part of a Bond film, have been mostly borrowed from previous pictures. And the Bond lady in the film (Maryam d`Abo) is slight in build and in presence. She and Dalton are quite tentative and have no chemistry. In fact, tentativeness marks the entire production, save for the now-tired chase sequences. Maybe the filmmakers were trying to strike a middle ground between the glamor of the Connery Bond films and the dubious humor of the Moore Bonds. The result is a film that is not so much bad as mechanical and uptight.'

Janet Maslin in the New York Times was thankfully more complimentary to Dalton and the movie than Gene Siskel. 'Dalton, the latest successor to the role of James Bond, is well equipped for his new responsibilities. He has enough presence, the right debonair looks and the kind of energy that the Bond series has lately been lacking. If he radiates more thoughtfulness than the role requires, maybe that's just gravy. He's less ironic than Sean Connery, less insistently suave than Roger Moore. Instead, Mr. Dalton has his own brand of charm. His Bond is world-wearier than others, but perhaps also more inclined to take the long view (as well he might, after all these years). In any case, he has enthusiasm, good looks and novelty on his side. Dalton, while less rakish than his predecessors, handles the romantic subplot charmingly.'

One of the best reviews for Daylights and Timothy Dalton came from Rita Kempley in The Washington Post. 'The best Bond ever,' she wrote. 'He's as classy as the trademark tuxedo, as sleek as the Aston Martin. Like Bond's notorious martini, women who encounter his carved-granite good looks are shaken, not stirred.' Gary Russell in Starburst was also very impressed and wrote - 'If not the best Bond, then certainly up there with From Russia With Love, Eyes Only and On Her Majesty's Secret Service. The most impressive factor in the film, the one on which its success depends more than the story, is one Timothy Dalton, who is so damn good as James Bond you feel like asking where he's been since Connery left. Although he's only done this one [and there's still no confirmation he's signed for another] I feel safe to proclaim

Dalton the best of the four, and one that Ian Fleming would have approved of. All in all, The Living Daylights has paved the way for a further twenty-five years of good James Bond films, and that is largely due to Timothy Dalton, who deserves as much credit as possible.'

Alexander Walker in the Standard was not so impressed though and wrote - 'Timothy Dalton looks poorly served by John Glen, once a tight editor and now a slack director, and doesn't begin to share the joke with the audience the way that the other Bonds did. He looks as if he takes it all for real and dislikes much of it. Cubby Broccoli and his associates should start the Think Tank going for the film after this, and decide what kind of Bond they want, for at the moment they haven't got one.' Derek Malcolm was also rather lukewarm and wrote in The Guardian - 'You no longer expect more than you get, and by now are left noting only the fine tuning of the formula. Dalton hasn't the natural authority of Connery nor the facile charm of Moore, but George Lazenby he is not. It's an able first go in the circumstances, though perhaps it could do with a bit more humour.'

Victoria Mather in The Telegraph was more positive and wrote - 'All the traditional elements are in place and Dalton has restored a vital element to 007 - the very best of British, the amateur gentleman who is better than any professional. He is kinder, more human, charming and low-profile. For me he is Bond, James Bond.' Variety was also glowing in their praise of the film. 'The Living Daylights is just the ticket to mark James Bond's 25 years on the screen... This one will be tough to top... Pic isn't just a high-tech action replay with the usual ravishing visuals and ditto games. Everyone seems to have tried a little harder this time... Everyone seemed up for this one and it shows.'

Timothy Dalton said that when The Living Daylights came out he secretly slipped into a New York cinema so he could watch it with an audience. "I went to see The Living Daylights here in New York. I sneaked into the back of a theatre, because a movie is not finished when you finish shooting it or after postproduction. It's finished when an audience sees it, because that's who you're doing it for. Just like you can write an article, but you're not going to tuck it away in a draw. What good will it do? You write it for people to read, so a movie is only finished when people have seen it. So I snuck into the back, and I was overwhelmed by the pleasure and the delight that people were taking in that movie. They're very vocal in America. Much more than anywhere else, I think, in the world, and to see that response was so satisfying and made me feel so happy."

The Living Daylights grossed about $190 million worldwide. It was up against the teen vampire horror comedy The Lost Boys at the US box-office but had an $11 million weekend to claim the top spot. In the end, Daylights comfortably outgrossed the previous three Roger Moore films so EON and Cubby Broccoli could be happy that their new era seemed to have made a more than solid start. Dalton's Byronic good looks and moody charm in The Living Daylights briefly seemed set to position him as the definitive screen James Bond. Timothy Dalton was very happy with how The Living Daylights turned out. Becoming the new Bond is a potentially risky venture for an actor but things seemed to have gone well for Dalton. Bond fans were already anticipating his second film and wondering how many he might make. At a fit and athletic 41 years of age, Dalton seemed set to take James Bond well into the 1990s.

Timothy Dalton was understandably relieved at the generally positive reception to the Living Daylights. "Going into it," he said, "I knew some people preferred Sean Connery, and some people preferred Roger Moore, but I thought to myself, 'My God, what if nobody likes me?' It doesn't even matter if you make a good movie, what if they don't like you as Bond? I mean, the results ended up being lots of people really loved what I did, but I guess there were a lot of people wishing it was more like what Roger Moore was doing. But that's one of the perils of stepping into an institution and following in the footsteps of lots of famous people."

Pierce Brosnan said that he avoided The Living Daylights like the plague when it came out. It was simply too painful to be reminded of the film he was supposed to star in. Brosnan couldn't avoid the film forever though and said he eventually encountered Daylights while part of a captive audience on a plane! The Scottish actor David Robb (who was touted as a potential Bond himself in the 1970s) acted in a 1988 film called The Deceivers with Brosnan around this time. Robb later said that Brosnan was still fuming about losing out on James Bond and grumbled about it endlessly on the set between takes.

As usual with the release of a new James Bond film there were numerous magazine specials, a music video, and even a computer game. Domark produced a Living Daylights computer game for the Commodore 64 based on the film. The Daylights game got decent to mediocre reviews and also appeared on the Spectrum, BBC Micro, and even the Amiga in the end. Domark had previously released an atrocious C64 game for A View To A Kill a few years before but their Living Daylights game was at least a slight improvement over that hopeless effort. Nothing could be possibly as bad as Domark's A View To A Kill game. The Daylights game was a more cohesive affair but it still left something to be desired.

Licenced movie games for the C64 were always a hit or miss affair. Games companies loved having the rights to a game based on a film or television series because they could just slap the movie or television poster art on the box and use this to lure unsuspecting C64 gamers to their product. Gamers in a shop would suddenly notice a game based on something like Rambo or Airwolf and be naturally curious and tempted. A licenced game did not guarantee quality though. Some very shoddy and wonky games were masked by tempting film poster art on the box. For example, games based on Big Trouble in Little China and Knight Rider are among the worst C64 games of all time.

The promo text for the Daylights game went like this - 'Brad Whitaker international arms dealer and megalomaniac. Necros - his ruthless sidekick. Koskov, double dealing KGB General and the beautiful Kara, the sophisticated Czech cellist who wins the hero's heart. Match them against James Bond, renowned British Secret Agent (for whom love and death is a way of life) and you have all the ingredients for a super spy story and a great gripping games! This game is closely based on the all action film and coin-op Arcade game from Arcadia, but puts you into the action as you control James Bond through eight fast and furious levels. Moving from Gibraltar to Afghanistan, you encounter the SAS (friendly) and the KGB (not so friendly) enemy helicopters (very unfriendly!) and even a milkman with exploding bottles! Now go ahead and join James Bond - living on the edge!'

The Daylights game is a side scrolling third-person shooter in the vein of games of the era like Green Beret. Don't get too excited though as Green Beret (though annoyingly difficult) is vastly superior. In the Daylights game you move a cursor around to shoot people who appear not only in front of you but also to the side at the top of the screen. This is the sort of mechanic that games like Operation Wolf would later deploy - but without the side scrolling. The problem in the Daylights game is that the mix of this mechanic with side scrolling is awkward and difficult to control. This mash up of different mechanics (including using the cursor to choose which direction to go) sounds ambitious for the time but the execution is quite crude. No other C64 game tried to copy the eccentric mechanics of the Daylights game and that probably tells you all you need to know about how successful it was.

As a white shirted pixel Timothy Dalton, you fight your way through eight levels (Gibraltar, The Lenin People's Music Conservatory, The Pipeline, The Mansion House, The Fairground, Tangiers, The Military Complex, Whitaker's House) to complete your mission in the Daylights game. Bond can run, duck, jump and use weapons created by Q (including the Ghetto Blaster) and also take out enemies with his trusted

Walther PPK. Although the controls are fiddly, the Daylights game is not a completely terrible experience and far from the worst licenced game of this era.

One of the main problems with Domark's A View To A Kill Game was that it was really three completely different mini-games in one package and none of these sections were satisfying in their own right (in fact, the first part in particular where you are supposed to be driving around Paris, was absolutely terrible). The Living Daylights game is at least quite breezy and fast moving in comparison and has a consistent concept behind it. The Living Daylights wants to keep things simple and be an arcade game where you are constantly shooting things all the way through. The gameplay never changes.

Domark's A View To A Kill game tried to be a driving game, a puzzle game, and (finally) a platform game but none of these individual sections worked and the game felt like it was all over the place and had bitten off more than it could chew. The main criticism of the Daylights game was that it was merely a Missile Command clone (in that you follow a cursor to shoot targets which appear) dressed up in different graphics. The Daylights game becomes a little samey after a while but at least some effort is made to make the various backdrops look different. It's a shame though that the game doesn't include Kara and there is no car section either.

As ever with C64 games, the James Bond theme is comically mangled by the audio technology of the time. Bond is supplied with various different weapons in the game by Q. These include a bazooka and crossbow. While the playability and durability of the Daylights game is questionable, at the very least you can say that a modicum of effort went into it. The Living Daylights game doesn't feel like a completely lazy cash grab but you probably haven't missed out on an awful lot if you've never played it. It's nice though to have a Timothy Dalton Bond video game - however primitive it might seem today in a world of games like Doom Eternal.

While he waited for his second Bond film to come around and fall into place, Timothy Dalton kept busy by making Hawks - a little known 1988 film directed by Robert Ellis Miller. In the film two terminally ill cancer patients in a London hospital - a lawyer named Bancroft (Dalton) and a young American football player named Deckermensky (Anthony Edwards) - decide to steal an ambulance and head for an Amsterdam brothel for one last adventure before they die. Bancroft believes they are hawks in a world of pigeons and should go out on their own terms rather than ebb away in the ordered confines of a hospital with its rules and conventions. Once in the Netherlands, they meet a pair of mismatched women (played by Camille Coduri and Janet McTeer) who teach them a few lessons about life in a roundabout way.

Hawks was a very personal project to Dalton and a film he has always spoken highly of. Dalton said of the film - "Hawks deals with the subject of extraordinary relevance: Why does it take a crisis to make you realize how bloody precious life is? Unfortunately, it's about cancer, which is a not a word the film business thinks of as being particularly commercial. Still, doing the first Bond film enabled me to get Hawks made. Doing the Bond film helped the O'Neill play find an audience. This is a commercial business. If you have a commercial success, you have enhanced viability."

Hawks sounds incredibly depressing on the face of it but turns out to be a pleasantly uplifting experience in the end with some good black humour and an enthusiastic performance by Dalton as Bancroft. Dalton made this in between his two James Bond films and one can admire his pluck in avoiding typecasting and taking on something he knew full well wasn't the most commercial enterprise in the world. You wouldn't quite say that Dalton is trying to avoid 007 typecasting (he'd only made one Bond film at the time!) but he's patently enjoying the chance to do something that is nothing at all like James Bond and The Living Daylights. Timothy Dalton seemed to be somewhat typecast in period costume dramas before Bond so with Hawks (and indeed The Living Daylights) it was nice to see him in the present day!

Hawks seems to be an incredibly obscure film today (I personally can't recall ever encountering this film on television) and is a fairly modest affair in terms of production values but it isn't as bleak as the subject matter might suggest and always manages to remain sufficiently interesting and engaging enough to hold your interest. Dalton gives a committed performance as the eccentric and frustrated Bancroft and Anthony Edwards (a likeable actor who was in many films during this period) is also good in the film. Dalton is sometimes a trifle theatrical in film roles (this an unavoidable by-product of his stage work I suppose) but was always a much more versatile actor than he ever got credit for. He nails the bitterness that Bancroft tries to contain but allows to come to the surface - especially in the hospital scenes.

Timothy Dalton has certain mannerisms and quirks as an actor which he carries into all of his roles but even so he's quite successful here at disappearing into the character of Bancroft to the point where you sort of forget that he's Timothy Dalton or James Bond. It does help I suppose that he sports a woolly hat for most of the film! Hawks benefits too from the fact that it never feels gratuitously manipulative or saccharine. You feel like the film does try and earn its more emotional moments. In some ways this is like an early British version of The Bucket List.

The story in Hawks is credited to Barry Gibb - who also supplies the enjoyably dated eighties soundtrack. Roy Clarke, a veteran writer of many British sitcoms, wrote the screenplay. Dalton and Edwards work well together as the lead characters - Edwards the more dubious one at first regarding Bancroft's desire to throw out the rule book and live the remainder of his life in the way he wants, even if it flies in the face of established conventions. The gender politics of the film are a little dated but Camille Coduri and Janet McTeer make the most of their parts as the two women our heroes meet in on their travels. It's an unavoidably sad film at times but very watchable and quite moving in its best moments. Hawks is definitely a film that deserved a slightly bigger audience than it ever received.

As the James Bond team began to prepare for Timothy Dalton's second film, they faced the familiar problem of how to keep Bond relevant and at the forefront of action adventure movies. The year that The Living Daylights came out saw Lethal Weapon and Robocop released. 1988 saw the release of Die Hard - which completely raised the bar when it came to action films. It was no easy task for the Bond team to keep up with the competition but then this had been the case for many decades. Bond was essentially the first action franchise. It invented a whole new genre. Without the James Bond franchise there would have been no Indiana Jones, no Jason Bourne, no Derek Flint, and no Ethan Hunt. Everyone from Steven Spielberg to James Cameron to Christopher Nolan was hugely influenced by the Bond films.

The deadpan quips by Arnold Schwarzenegger in his classic action films were lifted directly from Sean Connery's Bond. The Bond series was also hugely influential in the many villains we've seen in action films through the decades. Alan Rickman's Hans Gruber in Die Hard is like the best Bond villain we never got. Shih Kien as the steel handed baddie Han in Enter the Dragon is patently a Bond inspired villain. Inevitably, though once a trend setter, the Bond series eventually became deluged with competition in the vey genre it could claim (with some justification) to have invented. Sure there were cliffhanger serials and adventure romps before 007 but James Bond was the first movie series to do it on a huge budget and introduce the modern action tropes we still in evidence in the cinema of today.

It was unavoidable in the end then that the Bond franchise would itself start to be inspired by other films. Live and Let Die was influenced by the Blaxploitation genre (one could argue too that Live and Let Die is the only Bond movie that is influenced by the horror genre). The Man with the Golden Gun has some kung-fu scenes in deference to the Bruce Lee phenomenon. Moonraker was patently inspired by Kubrick's 2001 and Star Wars. The influence of Raiders of the Lost Ark is evident in some of the stunts in the early 1980s Bond films. The Daniel Craig reboot was later heavily influenced by the Jason Bourne films. Quantum of Solace took the Bourne influence to extremes and even tried to mimic the obstreperous camera and editing style of Paul Greengrass.

The Bond franchise has had to compete with an eclectic and constant number of action films and franchises over the decades. Many of these films and franchises were inspired by Bond themselves. The list of films and franchises the Bond series, over many decades, has had to keep pace with is endless and varied. Dirty Harry, Enter the Dragon, Rambo, Lethal Weapon, Superman, Die Hard, Mad Max, Arnold Schwarzenegger movies, John Woo, Speed, Mission Impossible, Batman, The Matrix, Derek Flint, Matt Helm, Bulldog Drummond, Remo Williams, The Long Kiss Goodnight, Lara Croft, xXx, Jack Ryan, Jackie Chan, Stormbreaker, The Peacemaker, Fast and the Furious, Marvel, John Wick, Taken. No other franchise or action character though has been as enduring as James Bond.

Bond did invent the big budget action franchise but even Cubby Broccoli and Harry Saltzman had their own influences in 1962. The Bond series was heavily influenced by Alfred Hitchcock's masterful 1959 suspense thriller North By Northwest. North By Northwest was in many ways the first James Bond film. It has a suave leading man, adventure, action, varied locations, panache, urbane villains, suggestive humour. The helicopter sequence in From Russia With Love is clearly inspired the cropdusting sequence in North By Northwest. The Bond producers were so inspired by North By Northwest that they even tried to persuade Cary Grant (who was a friend of Cubby Broccoli) to play James Bond in Dr No. Grant, who was in his early sixties at the time, declined this offer though because he felt he was too old for the part.

Bond fans didn't have to wait long for Bond 16 to begin the path to production. Remarkable as it might seem today, in that era a James Bond film was released every two years. Nowadays you never have the faintest idea when EON will deliver the next film! The longs gaps between the Daniel Craig films after Quantum of Solace became sort of ridiculous in the end. It was after Quantum that the frustration began. Bond fans then had to wait four years for the next entry - Skyfall. Fans then had to wait three years for Spectre. Fans were then expected to wait FIVE years for Bond 25 - until the coronavirus threatened to make this wait even longer. Cubby Broccoli would not have sat on his thumbs for years waiting for a Bond actor to decide if he wanted to come back or not in the way that Barbara Broccoli did with Daniel Craig and Bond 25. Cubby would have simply recast the part and got the cameras rolling again.

Although the script for The Living Daylights had been approached in a somewhat generic way because it was uncertain who would play Bond (and for a time also assumed that Pierce Brosnan would play Bond), the story for the next film was developed in a way to tailor it to Timothy Dalton's strengths. Both Dalton and the writers wanted the next film to be tougher and a bit more harder edged than The Living Daylights. "Dalton was more in the Connery mold so we had to tailor the scripts," said John Glen. "Roger was so humorous, and we tended to make all these films verging on comedy. They were very light situations – that was done purposely. When Timothy came on the scene, we had a fine Shakespearean actor, but he probably didn't have the humor that Roger had so we tailored the scripts accordingly. We made them slightly blacker or darker, in the sense that we wanted more dramatic situations. He was more ruthless and more of the original Bond and that was what we were trying to get back to."

The early plan was to shoot the new Bond film in China and two story treatments (which included a motorbike chase along the Great Wall) were written with this in mind. Unfortunately though the success of the film The Last Emporer nixed this plan and made the idea of going to China feel far less novel or fresh. In the end it was decided to give the next film a more tropical setting and Michael G. Wilson, initially working with Richard Maibaum but then working alone after a writer's strike, came up with a story that was inspired by Akira Kurosawa's Yojimbo (which in turn inspired films like A Fistful of Dollars). The idea was that Bond would play the villains off against one another to extract revenge for an attack on Felix Leiter. Wilson felt that 'revenge mission' story would be a good mesh for Timothy Dalton's darker take on James Bond.

Because of a change in the tax system in Britain, the film would be shot at Estudios Churubusco in Mexico City rather than Pinewood. Pinewood is a film and television studio located in the village of Iver Heath in Buckinghamshire. 'The studio opened on 30 September 1936,' wrote The Guardian, 'with owners Sir Charles Boot and J Arthur Rank inspired by Hollywood to create a thriving British film industry, a desire that led to a series of mergers with other studios over the years - the first in 1938, when Pinewood took over Alexander Korda's Denham Studios. Pinewood quickly established itself as a location for great British films. Pinewood's greatest association, however, is with the James Bond franchise. The first film, Dr No, was shot there in 1962, and despite fires destroying sets in 1984 and 2006, Bond films have continued to be filmed at the studio. The Bond stage was rebuilt in 1985, the year before Pinewood's 50th birthday, and renamed the Albert R. Broccoli Bond stage in honour of the 007 producer.'

This decision not to use Pinewood, while logical from the point of view of finances and the needs of the script for a tropical setting, did though run the risk of losing some Bond 'residue' when it came to tradition and atmosphere. If anywhere can be called the physical home of James Bond it is surely Pinewood. The irony is that because of logistical problems in Mexico, the film wouldn't actually have cost any more money if it had been based at Pinewood. Timothy Dalton later said he got rather homesick during the long shoot in Mexico and often wished he could go home and have a pint of beer in a pub! Sadly, the thin air of the Mexican locations caused Cubby Broccoli to suffer from breathing problems. He had to leave the production in the end and couldn't return. The pollution and high-altitude turned out to be something of an ordeal for the rest of the crew too.

CHAPTER SEVEN

Bond 16 would be the first Bond film not to have an original Fleming title (although there were still unused Fleming titles hanging around like Risico, The Property of a Lady, and Quantum of Solace). The original title of Timothy Dalton's second Bond film was License Revoked. A poster bearing this title appeared at the Cannes Film Festival. On the first day of shooting, Cubby Broccoli was pictured holding a slate which clearly says License Revoked. However, when market research suggested that the general public didn't know what the word 'revoked' meant this title was dropped in favour of Licence To Kill (a title which obviously adopted the British spelling). Believe it or not, one of the main reasons why License Revoked was jettisoned as a title was that many Americans associated the word 'revoked' with driving licences!

John Glen was asked back to direct Licence To Kill and he later confessed he was surprised to be brought back again. After four Bond films in succession, Glen had assumed that EON might try and freshen things up with a new director for Dalton's second picture. Cubby Broccoli obviously had a lot of trust and faith in Glen though and saw no reason to make a change at this point. The Living Daylights had proven that Glen was perfectly capable of making a less jovial type of Bond film. John Glen said he was very annoyed at the title change because License Revoked (or Licence Revoked as it might have become) was perfect for the story they were going to tell. Glen felt that Licence To Kill was very generic and lazy in comparison.

There was some speculation at the time that Dalton's second film might borrow some plot threads from the James Bond continuation novels written by John Gardner. However this speculation turned out to be misplaced. While the Bond films continue to mine plot threads, scenes, and character names from the Fleming books, EON have never shown much interest in openly adapting anything from the continuation novels.

This was a slight shame because many Bond fans feel that Colonel Sun (where M is kidnapped) by Kingsley Amis would have made a terrific basis for a Timothy Dalton Bond film.

The script for Licence To Kill borrowed a few elements from the Fleming short story The Hildebrand Rarity. The Hildebrand Rarity appeared in the 1960 short story collection For Your Eyes Only. In the story, while on holiday in the Seychelles, Bond falls in with dubious millionaire Milton Krest and is persuaded to join a search for a rare spiked fish known as The Hildebrand Rarity which Krest must find as part of a tax dodge. Krest beats his wife with a whip (Franz Sanchez has a similar habit in Licence To Kill) and poisons countless fish looking for The Hildebrand Rarity and the millionaire will be lucky to survive the boat trip without getting his comeuppance.

The Hildebrand Rarity has a rich exotic atmosphere that makes you feel as if you are on the boat yourself in these languid and sun-drenched Indian Ocean waters. The Hildebrand Rarity is not the most exciting Bond adventure ever to make it into print but it works quite nicely as a reverse murder mystery and certainly has a memorable method of death for one character. One can see some elements in this story that grace Licence To Kill - not least having a character called Milton Krest.

Licence To Kill also borrows from Ian Fleming's shark festooned 1954 novel Live and Let Die - specifically the attack on Felix Leiter. Sadly though, the gripping sequence where Bond and Solitaire are tied up and face the prospect of being keelhauled over coral underwater (which would have made a great scene for Licence To Kill) had already been adapted in the 1981 Roger Moore film For Your Eyes Only.

The fictional Republic of Isthmus in Licence To Kill is based on Panama. The villain Franz Sanchez is based on Colombian drug lord and narcoterrorist Pablo Escobar. John Glen suggested Robert Davi as the villain Franz Sanchez after watching him a TV film. "I was looking for a villain who could be the physical equal of Tim's Bond, in much the same way Robert Shaw had been the equal of Sean Connery in From Russia With Love. The balance between hero and villain fascinates me and Robert Davi played the villainous side of the equation perfectly." Davi had appeared in films like Raw Deal, Die Hard, and The Goonies. Davi was delighted to be in a Bond film and even helped test potential the Bond Girls by playing 007 in auditions when Timothy Dalton was unavailable.

Of his casting, Robert Davi said - "Tina Broccoli was a fan of mine from Goonies and she thought I would get along with Cubby. So she set up a dinner with Cubby and Dana. Cubby and I were both born in Astoria, New York and of Italian descent, this brought us immediately close. About a year later I had done Terrorist on Trial. I had gotten tremendous critical acclaim and was on the cover of all the entertainment sections of the newspapers. This attention, and having met me, had made Cubby put on TOT. It so happened Richard Maibaum also was watching it and had called Cubby to put it on. Cubby said, "I'm watching it." Richard said, "That's the next Bond Villain!" Cubby said, "I think so too." I was called to meet Cubby, Michael Wilson and John Glenn the next day! And offered the part."

There were a lot of stories in the media that Cubby Broccoli had offered the part of the villain to the musician Gene Simmons of Kiss but this obviously didn't transpire in the end. The Cuban-born Venezuelan-American actress Maria Conchita Alonso (who unsuccessfully auditioned for the part of Fatima Blush in Never Say Never Again) was the original choice for the part of Lupe Lamora. However, after accepting the part, Alonso then had a change of heart and dropped out of the film.

Maria Conchita Alonso's departure led to fresh auditions and a dozen or so candidates were tested. The American model Talisa Soto, who had only a few acting credits at the time, was chosen after Davi said she was the most beautiful of the women they had tested. Soto later said that Lupe was much tougher and more morally dubious in the original script and that the character was changed and softened somewhat. "Lupe was truly a villain at first, but as we were working there were rewrites. They decided to soften her up and make her fall in love with James Bond."

One of the first people that director John Glen talked to for the part of Pam Bouvier was Sharon Stone. At the time, Stone was not yet a star and her CV consisted of supporting appearances in films like King Solomon's Mines, Allan Quatermain and the Lost City of Gold, Action Jackson, and Police Academy 4: Citizens on Patrol. Stone was obviously not chosen in the end though. The American model and actress Carey Lowell was eventually chosen to play Pam Bouvier in the film. Unlike Dalton's first film, Bond would have two love interests in Licence To Kill. Carey Lowell said she didn't know that much about Bond films when she got the part so for her research she simply started renting Bond movies from the video store to watch! The script wasn't finished when Carey Lowell auditioned so she did her test reading lines from A View To A Kill.

Carey Lowell was amazed at the attention she suddenly received after her casting and quickly realised that Bond was a worldwide phenomenon that would probably overshadow anything she ever went on to do. "I'm just amazed by the following for the Bond films," she told Cinefantastique. "I don't think I comprehended how much attention this film would get. It's a little overwhelming. It's very exciting as well to be in the company of the people who came before me-Sean Connery and the women. I had somebody the other day ask me how does it feel to know you're going to be in book indexes one day? It feels pretty good."

John Rhys-Davies was offered a chance to return as General Pushkin in Licence To Kill but he declined the offer because he was too busy shooting Indiana Jones and the Last Crusade. One of the most surprising additions to the cast was the crooner Wayne Newton as the TV evangelist Joe Butcher. Newton had apparently contacted Cubby Broccoli and said he'd always wanted to be in a Bond film. Broccoli granted his wish. Newton based Joe Butcher on Jimmy Swaggart. Jimmy Swaggart is an American Pentecostal evangelist who has been on TV and radio for years. Newton ad-libbed much of Joe Butcher's dialogue in Licence To Kill.

Highly dependable and experienced American actors Anthony Zerbe, Don Stroud, Everett McGill, and Frank McRae were also given roles in the film and you certainly couldn't accuse John Glen and EON of not keeping an eye on up and coming talent because they cast a 21 year-old Benicio del Toro as the unhinged henchman of Sanchez. The MI6 team of Robert Brown, Caroline Bliss, Desmond Llewelyn were all back and Anthony Starke was cast as the young financial whizzkid assistant of Sanchez. Grand L. Bush, who appeared in Die Hard with Robert Davi, was given a small role in Licence To Kill as a DEA agent.

Desmond Llewelyn was delighted at the expanded role promised for Q in Licence To Kill and later said he made more money from this Bond picture than any of the others. Desmond Llewelyn said that, in his view, Timothy Dalton was a fantastic actor who had made Bond feel more like a real person. Caroline Bliss fared less well than Llewelyn in Licence To Kill. Moneypenny is in the film for about ten seconds and Bliss didn't even get to play a scene with Timothy Dalton!

The biggest surprise in the cast was the return of David Hedison as Felix Leiter - a role he had previously played in Live and Let Die alongside Roger Moore in 1973. At 61, Hedison was nearly twenty years older than Timothy Dalton so this casting was somewhat eccentric to say the least. No one was more surprised than Hedison himself at his return! Hedison had bumped into Cubby and Dana Broccoli at the Bistro Gardens in Beverly Hills and several weeks later got a call from John Glen inviting him to be in the film. Hedison was happy to accept this unexpected chance to be in a James

Bond film again.

John Glen had reservations about casting Hedison because of his age but Cubby Broccoli wanted Hedison so that was that. Glen's reservations were rather confirmed when Hedison injured both his knees shooting the PTS moment where Leiter and Bond arrive back at the church (just in time for Leiter's wedding) by parachute. Priscilla Barnes (already a TV veteran and later to become a familiar face in low-budget horror movies) was cast as Della - the doomed wife of Felix. Barnes had previously starred in the little seen 1980 anthology film Sunday Lovers with Roger Moore.

The title song for Licence To Kill was originally supposed to be done by Eric Clapton. There was apparently a plan to eschew a traditional title song and have a reworked version of the Bond theme over the titles. This would have been an interesting approach. The Bond franchise hasn't had a purely instrumental theme since On Her Majesty's Secret Service. One might argue that given how bland some of the recent Bond theme songs have been, an upbeat instrumental piece in the vein of OHMSS might be rather novel and exciting. Obviously, Eric Clapton didn't do the theme music for Bond 16 in the end though. Gladys Knight was instead chosen to sing a more traditional (and, as it turned out) enjoyably Bondian song.

The costume department wanted to put Bond in pastel colours and designer clothes in Licence To Kill but Timothy Dalton didn't like this plan and wanted to wear plainer clothes in the film. Dalton argued that Bond was a spy who had gone rogue so should wear clothes that didn't make him stand out! "The clothes say so much about Bond," said Dalton. "He's got a naval background, so he needs a strong, simple colour like dark blue." It was a far cry from Roger Moore's Bond - who was always impeccably attired (even in the desert!) and seemed to be recognised all over the world! Dalton's Bond in Licence To Kill is probably the most casual and down to earth we've ever seen when it comes to fashion.

Timothy Dalton fought his corner on the set of Licence To Kill and not just when it came to clothes. Dalton insisted that Bond should not sleep with Lupe early in the film (as had been planned) because Lupe had been exploited by men and it would seem as if Bond was just using her in the same way. Dalton argued that Bond should be faithful to Pam and resist the attentions of Lupe. He felt this is what Fleming's Bond would done. This was obviously not something in the tradition of the Cinematic Bond. Sean Connery's Bond would have seduced both Pam and Lupe early on in the film and had no qualms whatsoever! "Tim is a man with passion," said Michael G. Wilson of disagreements on the set of Licence To Kill. He expresses himself very frankly. I never take offence because I can express myself with some passion too."

Licence To Kill had a budget of $32 million (which ended up at $36 million in the end) and principal photography ran from the 18th of July to the 18th of November 1988. In addition to Mexico, filming took place in the Florida Keys. The Seven Mile Bridge, where Sanchez escapes after the police van crashes into the sea, was later used in the 1994 James Cameron spy adventure film True Lies. The mansion belonging to Sanchez in the movie was owned by friends of Cubby Broccoli. In return for a donation to a charity of their choice, Broccoli was given permission to use the house in Licence To Kill.

Timothy Dalton once again impressed the stunt crew by his willingness to do as many stunts as possible. That's really Dalton being winched below the helicopter and also Dalton hanging on that tanker truck. Barbara Broccoli was the producer on the big tanker chase and impressed everyone with her organisation and authority. You might say that Barbara finished her apprenticeship on the Dalton films. When the series returned in the 1990s several years later, Barbara Broccoli was much more powerful in EON and a full fledged producer. The moment in the tanker chase when Bond jumps from Pam's plane to the truck had to be delayed for four days because the weather wasn't good.

In an interview many years later, Timothy Dalton said he only got the script for Licence To Kill about two weeks before it began shooting. This was something that clearly irritated him as he felt it didn't give him enough time to prepare for the movie. This fact clearly illustrates that Dalton had minimal creative control. The only Bond actor who seems to have exerted a creative control over the franchise is Daniel Craig. Craig practically became a co-producer on his movies and enjoyed considerable input into the scripts, choice of writers, choice of director, and even the artist to do the theme song. Timothy Dalton and Pierce Brosnan could only dream of such influence. A frustrated Brosnan couldn't even persuade the producers to hire Monica Belluci rather than Teri Hatcher for Tomorrow Never Dies.

In a set visit to Licence To Kill, Garth Pearce noted that Timothy Dalton hadn't let becoming James Bond change him at all as a person. Dalton still lived in the same modest house he'd had since before he became Bond and still did all his own shopping. "Why should I change?" said Dalton. "I can walk around the streets, drink a pint without being bothered too much and still go shopping for my baked beans. I can't see how I can begin to play other roles if I'm so far removed from life I never meet the kind of people I am playing." Dalton said he hardly did anything apart from acting though did admit that he enjoyed a game of poker now and again.

Timothy Dalton certainly found himself in the wars shooting Licence To Kill. At one point Benicio del Toro cut Dalton's hand quite badly shooting a scene where Bond is captured but Dalton - ever the trooper - was soon back on the set to finish the scene. Dalton said that it was extremely rough shooting some of the explosive tanker chase scenes (not to mention the climax where sets light to Felix - triggering a massive explosion) and that it rather put him off doing stunts in the future.

The shoot was even tougher for Dalton than The Living

Daylights and it seems a few tempers were frayed by the end of the production. The relationship between Dalton and John Glen was somewhat fractious at the conclusion of the shoot. "Things ended in a bit of a sour atmosphere, unfortunately," wrote John Glen of Licence To Kill in his memoir. "I was feeling a little unwell and Tim wasn't in the best of moods either. The whole thing was a bit of an ordeal and Tim and I had a bit of a slanging match across the pool. I don't know whether to put it down to tiredness at the end of the schedule or the accumulated tension of what had been an unusually arduous shoot."

CHAPTER EIGHT

Licence To Kill might well be the most divisive Bond film ever made. I have seen Bond blogs where this movie is rated as the worst James Bond film ever made (a view that personally baffles me!) and dismissed as looking like a cheap television movie. There are others though who feel it is criminally underrated. As Raymond Benson said - "It boggles my mind that Licence to Kill is so controversial. There's really more of a true Ian Fleming story in that script than in most of the post-60s Bond movies." Licence To Kill is generally seen as the film where Timothy Dalton crashed the Bond franchise and left it stranded on some desolate rocks but this is grossly unfair and simplistic. Licence To Kill was very profitable outside of the United States and Timothy Dalton would almost certainly have played 007 a few more times had not the litigation (of which more later) quagmire occurred.

Licence To Kill doubles down on the more grounded aura of The Living Daylights and makes 007 even more human. The villain is also noticeably more topical and real world than we are used to in Bond films. Even Truman-Lodge, Sanchez's young financial advisor, is a nod to insider trading scandals of the era. Licence To Kill has many elements seemingly plucked from the newspapers of 1988. The basic plot has Bond going rogue and seeking revenge on Franz Sanchez - the boss of a fictional Latin American country. Sanchez is not interested in world domination or the usual preoccupation of Bond villains past. He is only interested in controlling the drugs trade and maintaining his power in Isthmus.

The film begins with Bond on his way to the wedding of Felix Leiter and Della. Felix is given an unexpected chance though to capture the drug baron Sanchez and so decides to take advantage of this. Bond insists on tagging along - but only as an 'observer' stipulates Felix. Bond however is not a man to take a back seat in any situation and he inevitably ends up capturing Felix by dangling from a helicopter and attaching a cable to the light aircraft Sanchez is trying to escape in.

The PTS stunt is not tremendously spectacular compared to previous Bond films but it's quite nice to see Bond and Leiter working together. It helps that we can plainly see that it is really Timothy Dalton dangling from the DEA helicopter and so the stunt has more realism because it is Bond (and not an obvious stuntman) who is there in the thick of the action. That's a lovely moment when Felix and Bond parachute down to the church in time for the wedding. The PTS gives us our first look at Sanchez and Robert Davi makes a striking first impression. He is appropriately cold and sadistic as the baddie. We also get our first look at Talisa Soto as Lupe. Soto is one of the most stunning Bond Girls of any era and while not exactly Diana Rigg in the acting department she is competent enough with what she is given to do.

Maurice Binder's title sequence (which would be his last) is an improvement on A View To A Kill and The Living Daylights. The title sequence has a photography theme (with cameras beginning and ending the sequence) and also uses Former Playboy Playmate Diane Hsu to good effect. Hsu also has a small role in the film as Hong Kong Narcotics Agent Loti. Gladys Knight's theme song (composed by by Narada Michael Walden, Jeffrey Cohen and Walter Afanasieff) is superb and deliberately uses the opening bars to Goldfinger for that extra Bond residue. I personally find the theme song for Licence To Kill more satisfying than any of the theme songs used for the Brosnan or Craig films. By the way, the music video for Licence To Kill was directed by the very talented Daniel Kleinman - who would later replace Maurice Binder as the title credits designer.

Sanchez is sprung from his prison van and rescued by frogman after it crashes into the sea. This is a pretty good sequence and might have inspired a similar scene in the recent Mission Impossible - Fallout. John Glen later complained that the static budgets of the Bond films at this time made it difficult to stage all the action in Licence To Kill but you never really get this impression watching the film. One could argue though that the wedding scenes at the start of the movie are a trifle television movie in scope. John Glen clearly wanted to just get this stuff in the bank as quickly as possible and move onto the more complex sequences on his slate.

David Hedison is clearly on the old side to play Leiter to Dalton's Bond but he's not bad. Dalton and Hedison have more chemistry than John Terry and Dalton had in Daylights - although, obviously, Hedison had the advantage of a much more expanded role than Terry's cameo. The scene where Sanchez feeds Leiter to a shark is rather grim and violent for Bond (you can see how Licence To Kill got a 15 certificate in Britain) but it does help establish Sanchez as a ruthless villain. Usually a Bond villain will explain his evil plans in great detail but never get around to half of them. Sanchez is more to the point though. One can't help feeling that the more sadistic nature of the villain in Licence To Kill is an attempt by EON to keep up with the competition. Films like Robocop and Die Hard had terrific (and in the case of Robocop, very nasty) villains

'No villain matches Sanchez for menace,' wrote Den of Geek in a retrospective article about Licence To Kill. 'If he uncovered Bond, he would kill Bond. Simple as that. Not quite 'why don't you just shoot him' because Sanchez wouldn't just shoot him. He'd exact a far nastier retribution. But exact it he would. No locking Bond in a windowed room, no escorting Bond round the pad and feeding him dinner, no leaving Bond in a perilous situation and then departing for tea. If Sanchez wanted Bond dead, Bond would be killed. Thoroughly. Such ruthlessness is refreshing and admirable on the writers' behalf. Franz Sanchez is unquestionably the great forgotten villain of the franchise. He possesses all the vital characteristics: charm, intelligence, ruthlessness.'

Some critics felt that the plot of Licence To Kill didn't have much ambition but I'm not quite sure what they meant by that. The villain is less ambitious in his status and motivation than past Bond villains but the story (while not exactly original) is at least something different from the usual Bond formula in that Bond has gone rogue and is trying to agitate the empire of a villain from the inside. The story in Licence To Kill is a mildly bold gambit for the franchise and taken on those terms not lacking in ambition at all.

The wedding scenes give Dalton some welcome lighter moments before the revenge plot kicks in. One interesting thing they used to do in Bond films that connected the actors was to reference the death of Bond's wife in On Her Majesty's Secret Service. Roger Moore's Bond is noticeably touchy in The Spy Who Loved Me when Barbara Bach as Anya Amasova mentions that he was once married. As we noted, the PTS of For Your Eyes Only begins with Roger's Bond placing flowers on the grave of his wife (this scene was actually written for a new Bond actor because they didn't think Roger was coming back). It was left in though and provides a nice little 'human' moment for Roger's Bond.

In Licence To Kill, Timothy Dalton smiles weakly and is reluctant to accept a garter from Della when she tells him that he'll be the next to get married. These little moments in the Moore and Dalton films were a nice touch and connected the cinematic Bonds in a very understated but effective way. Dalton's reluctant acceptance of the garter is a touching moment. Timothy was considered for On Her Majesty's Secret Service so it isn't too much of a stretch to believe he lost his wife "a long time ago" as a young agent. By the time of the Brosnan and Craig (a reboot anyway) films, the references to Bond's wife were dropped. Too much time had passed.

Dalton is a trifle over the top conveying Bond's grief at finding Della and this scene isn't helped by Michael Kamen's score. Kamen, like David Arnold, tends to 'overscore' certain moments to the point where the score becomes too obtrusive. John Barry was much more slick when to came to providing a perfect sonic backdrop. Dalton's Bond is very cold and ruthless in this film. This is most apparent when he murders Killifer.

Bond is so determined in this film he even punches his way out of a meeting with M! This scene works quite well because Bond's actions are logical. He's expecting to be restrained, probably drugged, and put back on a plane to London.

The concept of Bond going rogue on a 'personal' mission is old hat these days (it seems to feature in most the Craig films!) but at the time of Licence To Kill it was quite a radical departure from the Bond formula. There are some nice touches in the early part of the film, like the way Bond has to do some old fashioned detective work and break into an office to look for Leiter's contacts. The casting in Licence To Kill is sometimes mocked but I've never quite understood this mockery myself. Anthony Zerbe is terrific as the oleaginous Milton Krest and Benicio Del Torro is enjoyably unhinged as Dario. Frank McRae is also good as Leiter's friend Sharkey. It's great to see Christopher Neame too as Fallon, a snooty government operative who plans to 'ship' Bond back to London.

The main liabilities in the cast are Priscilla Barnes and Anthony Starke but neither of them have what you would describe as large roles. Wayne Newton, a strange piece of casting on the face of it, is actually pretty funny as Joe Butcher. You would imagine Newton is no stranger to telethons and he's certainly believable as a suave but crooked televangelist. The bar room brawl scene feels like it doesn't really belong in a Bond film but it's great that Dalton is clearly less reliant on a stuntman than the other Bond actors. I like the scene where we can see that it's clearly Dalton hanging onto the side of Lupe's speedboat.

Another thing I like about Licence To Kill is the casino scenes seem quite lavish. When they did a casino scene in the Brosnan films it never felt as stylish as the one in Licence To Kill. There are plenty of aquatic capers in Licence To Kill which hark back to classic Bonds like Thunderball. The water ski sequence is a lot of fun although you do wish it had a John Barry score to punch the action up even more. Dalton and Robert Davi are very good in their scenes together and the concept of Bond winning the villain's trust before trying to stop him is at least something a bit different. Sanchez is an excellent villain on the whole.

It should be noted that Licence To Kill was not the finest hour of the EON hairdressing department. Dalton's hair seems to change in every scene and it's simply too long at times. Dalton is also given huge sideburns which make him look somewhat odd when his hair is (for no apparent reason) awkwardly slicked back in the casino scenes. The frustrating thing about all of this that Dalton looked terrifically James Bondian a few years later with a shortish haircut in The Rocketeer. Dalton actually looks at his best in Licence To Kill near the end when he's on the phone to Felix and then jumps in the pool with Pam. It's one of the few times in the film where Timothy Dalton's hair looks like a professional has actually attended to it!

Licence To Kill is fairly light on gadgets but there are some decent ones all the same. Bond fans will be well aware that Bond's signature gun (the optical palm reader means that the firing mechanism will only respond to 007's grip) is an idea that was later 'borrowed' (stolen might be a better word) for the Sam Mendes Bond film Spectre. Carey Lowell is not bad at all as Pam and has some flickers of chemistry with Dalton. This is a Bond film though that is not really that concerned with the usual romantic interludes.

Bond's infiltration of the Wavecrest is sometimes cited as the sequence where some felt Dalton was becoming far too serious and grim. To mitigate the tone though, we have the arrival of Q in an enjoyable and amusing expanded role. I don't really understand people who say Licence To Kill has no sense of humour. Did they not notice the finest hour of Desmond Llewelyn? The death of Milton Krest in the decompression chamber is one of the nastiest in the series and had to undergo a few cuts. Licence To Kill is pretty grisly at times. Bond shoots someone with a speargun and the PTS makes it clear that Sanchez has the heart of Lupe's lover removed (though mercifully offscreen).

While you wouldn't want every Bond film to be like this it is sort of refreshing that they pushed the violence and sadism boat out here though and tried to shake the formula up. I don't think Licence To Kill is entirely successful and there are flaws but it's a brave film and largely a very entertaining one. The Olimpatec Meditation Institute is a good backdrop for a Bond film and I love the sequence where Bond is put on the conveyor belt. It's a classic cliffhanger sequence.

The scenes where Bond wakes up in the luxurious mansion of Sanchez are enjoyably surreal and Dalton is impressive in the way that he makes James Bond feel very realistic in some of these scenes. Dalton's Bond is not an indestructible superman. There are times in Licence To Kill when he makes mistakes or seems in over his head. The tanker chase sequence at the end is terrific and grand scale fun. The incredibly explosive death of Sanchez is also memorable.

Licence To Kill is a very entertaining film at its best. It has two memorable Bond women, a great villain, and some terrific stunts. While I still slightly prefer The Living Daylights, I still feel that Licence To Kill is the Bond franchise firing on most of its cylinders and an excellent movie. The weaknesses of the film are Michael Kamen's score and the locations - which eschew globetrotting and stick to Latin America and Florida.

James Bond films with a preponderance of American locations (like Diamonds Are Forever) sometimes lack some of the Bond residue of other pictures in the franchise. I suppose this is because there are so many Hollywood action and adventure films set in the United States that James Bond feels a little on the generic side when it does the same. We are simply too used to a more varied and far-flung range of locations in Bond films.

John Barry was unavailable for Licence To Kill because of medical problems and it's obviously a great shame that he didn't do this picture. Can you imagine Licence To Kill with a John Barry score? It would have immediately made the film at least 25% better and more Bondian! His replacement Michael Kamen was known for scoring films like Die Hard and Lethal Weapon. While his work on other pictures was good he never quite seems to feel at home in Licence To Kill scoring a Bond film. It is noticeable that his Licence To Kill score has dated much faster than John Barry's music. Even the gunbarrel music at the start of Licence To Kill lacks punch. Kamen's flamenco themed music for Licence To Kill is largely unmemorable. The closing song by (If You Asked Me) by Patti LaBelle is pleasant enough though.

One thing I don't concur with on Licence To Kill is that it was heavily inspired by the (then) popular television show Miami Vice (in which a pastel suited Don Johnson would chase drug barons around Florida in speedboats). Licence To Kill is much more in hoc to Fleming than Don Johnson! Licence To Kill is far from flawless and could have done with a trifle more humour for Bond but it is a rousing action adventure at its best with plenty of scenes that push the violence envelope for Bond. When Bond jumps into the pool with Pam at the end I feel a genuine sense of sadness that we never got to see Dalton play 007 at least one more time.

I've never quite understood the perception either that Licence To Kill is a cheap looking film. It is true that thanks to studio penny pinching the budget afforded to the film was not an upgrade on The Living Daylights but Licence To Kill did apparently cost $36 million to make in the end. The locations are expansive and the film never feels studio bound (in the way that the more lavishly praised Goldeneye occasionally did). The tanker chase looks like it cost an absolute fortune and there are numerous shenanigans involving planes, helicopters, ships, scuba diving, and boats.

Timothy Dalton's best moments in the film are when the speedboat breaks down and he negotiates with Pam and his scenes with Q. Bond is charmingly protective of Q in Licence

To Kill and treats him like a grandfather at times. Classic 'Dalton Bond' moments in the film are Dalton headbutting the goon in the Sanchez lab, telling Fallon to p*** off, and lacing subtext into ordering a vodka-martini. The script for Licence To Kill is patently not one that is striving to be funny and so the smattering of 'Bond quips' feel somewhat jarring at times. Dalton is clearly not as ease when he has to say lines like - "Looks like he came to a dead end!" Roger Moore could have made that quip funny but Dalton can't. What is missing is more understated humour. Some of the jokes in the film are a trifle on the nose (the Hemingway reference when Bond meets M for example).

One thing about Timothy Dalton's Bond I really like, and it is something that he rarely seems to get credit for, is connecting different qualities of the Cinematic Bond. Roger Moore was suave but he wasn't tough. Pierce Brosnan was handsome and looked the part but he lacked depth. Daniel Craig is tough and has depth but he isn't suave and doesn't have the archetypal James Bond looks. Timothy Dalton however managed to encompass a surprisingly large number of these qualities. Dalton could be tough AND suave. He had depth and subtext. Dalton also had (especially in The Living Daylights) the archetypal James Bond look in that he is tall, dark, and handsome.

Of course, all the Bond actors have had their strengths and weaknesses and Dalton was no different. Some believe that Timothy Dalton didn't have the screen presence and charisma of some of the other Bonds. It's all down to personal taste really. One would concede that most of the other Bond actors were better at humour than Dalton. Sean Connery is sort of exempt from this debate because he had almost every Bond cinematic quality in spades. The only thing Connery's Bond lacked was depth. Connery was perfectly capable of depth as an actor but his Bond was never written this way. As for Lazenby, well, he ticked a surprising amount of boxes too. He was tough, had a classic James Bond look, and was even given some depth thanks to the more human approach of OHMSS.

Like Dalton though, Lazenby wasn't a natural when it came to delivering a quip.

One quality I like in Dalton's Bond, and this quality is apparent in Licence To Kill, is vulnerability. This quality is very genuine when a desperate Bond asks Pam to help him fight Sanchez when their speedboat runs out of fuel. Because of these moments of vulnerability and the nature of Bond's mission (avenging the ghastly violent attack on Leiter) it is very easy to root for Bond in Licence To Kill. Although the Bond we see in Licence To Kill is sometimes quite angry he is also likeable and this means we feel more of a connection to the character.

In retrospect, Licence To Kill feels like a fascinating anomaly in the franchise, sandwiched as it is between the Roger Moore and Pierce Brosnan eras. Not even the Daniel Craig films have the grisly violent flourishes of Licence To Kill. Despite its high body count though, Licence To Kill is still fun. It has plenty of action and chases. As for accusations that Licence To Kill is too grim, I can understand why some might have this view but all the same it's not exactly an Ingmar Bergman film. Licence To Kill, for me, is still a good time. I always have fun when I watch it.

On the whole, out of the two Dalton films, I prefer Daylights because of the John Barry score, mix of locations, and the atypical restraint of the romantic elements. Timothy Dalton is also more natural in Daylights. Dalton is occasionally too one-note in Licence To Kill compared to his debut. Generally though I like Dalton in Licence To Kill and you could argue that the determined and decidedly not tongue-in-cheek Bond he portrays here serves as a very early blueprint for what they tried to do in the Daniel Craig era many years later.

CHAPTER NINE

John Glen and EON were greatly dismayed when Licence To Kill received a 15 certificate in Britain. Four different versions of the film were released with Britain and Europe getting the most watered down version (in that cuts were made to violent scenes). The death of Krest in the decompression chamber (where his head explodes!) was one scene that had to be trimmed. It must have been a slightly new experience for EON to grapple with censors in this fashion. The 15 certificate in Britain was a big blow because James Bond films had always traditionally been enjoyed by children.

In a 2012 interview, Barbara Broccoli reflected on realism and violence in Bond films and seemed to suggest that, in her view, Licence To Kill might have gone a little too far.

"When we did Licence to Kill, that was a lot more violent," she reflected. "It was the first one that got a 15-rating in the UK, and I think we overstepped the mark there, in terms of going a bit too far into the realism. So that's something we're always struggling with. When to be realistic, and if so, how realistic and how much."

Studio cost cutting also (much to the irritation of Cubby Broccoli) threatened to damage Licence To Kill before it had even been released. Robert Peak designed fantastic teaser illustration and art for Licence To Kill but it was all dumped for a cheaper and far less effective campaign. MGM also discarded a campaign created by advertising executive Don Smolen, who had worked in the publicity campaign for eight previous Bond films. Certainly, the North American poster for Licence To Kill that did emerge must rank as one of the worst posters ever produced for Bond and gives you little clue that it's even promoting a James Bond film! In a sign of the times, Dalton was featured in casual clothes in all the poster art. The lack of the traditional tux did make the art seem less Bondian and lacking in tradition.

Marketing is definitely something that the modern Bond films are very good at but Licence To Kill plainly dropped the ball. Licence To Kill was severely hamstrung by the penny pinching marketing campaign. The marketing on the Brosnan and Craig films was later excellent. When a Bond film is released today you would literally have to be living on another planet not to notice the marketing and promotional campaign. No stone is left unturned in the quest to inform audiences that Bond is back.

One very shrewd thing the Bond franchise did after Timothy Dalton era was move the release dates of the films to the winter rather than the summer. This has generally meant that Bond films will now open at a time when there is less competition at the box-office. It isn't always this simple (Tomorrow Never Dies famously found itself up against James Cameron's Titanic - but then who would have guessed that Titanic would be so insanely popular and make two billion dollars?) but, for the most part, opening Bond films around October or November has been a profitable strategy and new tradition for EON.

The tagline for Licence To Kill was - 'James Bond is out on his own and out for revenge and out for revenge.' The American trailer for Licence To Kill was good fun because they got Timothy Dalton in to shoot a few framing bits just for the trailer. Dalton frames the trailer by looking determined and angry in a black outfit and Bond's digital watch is used as a sort of countdown backdrop to the action. "When you get on his bad side your number is up!" went the voiceover. One might argue though that the marketing was somewhat overegging the 'oooh, he's really dangerous in this one' angle and losing some Bondian essence in the process.

John Gardner wrote the novelisation of Licence To Kill and had a dreadful time trying to tie the story in with the continuity of the Fleming novels (where Leiter suffered an identical shark attack in Live and Let Die). In the end Gardner rather brushed over the return of Milton Krest (from The Hildebrand Rarity) and had the shark attacking Leiter's false leg from the previous attack! The Felix Leiter in the Gardner continuity must rank as one of the unluckiest people in history to experience two identical shark attacks!

A graphic novel adaptation of Licence To Kill (by Mike Grell, Richard Ashford, Chuck Austen, Tom Yeates, and Stan Woch) was also released by Eclipse Books. This adaptation is nothing to write home about and is rather confusing to follow if you aren't very familiar with the film. The main problem with the graphic novel is that Timothy Dalton refused permission for his likeness to be used and the illustrations of James Bond are never consistent in the book. The visual depiction of Bond in the graphic novel frequently changes to the point you are occasionally confused as to who he is supposed to be! In one panel he actually looks like Dalton but in other panels he looks like the Daily Express Bond or even nothing like Bond at all. The Licence To kill graphic novel is probably one for curious completists only.

Timothy Dalton seemed very happy with Licence To Kill and said in an interview that it was a 'great leap forward' after Daylights. However, years later, Dalton would say he liked Daylights better than Licence To kill. Dalton did give one slightly gloomy interview when Licence To Kill was released where he said he feared Licence To Kill might be the last ever Bond film. He was obviously wrong about this but over the next several years Bond fans could be forgiven for feeling that his hunch was depressingly accurate! What might have prompted Dalton's gloomy prognosis is not known. Maybe he was just tired after a long and difficult shoot.

As with The Living Daylights, there was a computer game by Domark to tie in with Licence To kill. This game was released on both the Commodore 64 and the Amiga. The game is a top down vertical scrolling action shoot-em-up where you pursue Franz Sanchez through various levels. The game starts in the vein of other top down shooters like 1942. You control a helicopter and battle your way through Florida landscapes blasting anything in sight. The gameplay in the first level is sort of like Space Invaders except you can move the helicopter forward and back and have to shoot numerous ground targets in addition to other aircraft. It's nothing radical or amazing but competent enough as an undemanding shooting level to begin the game.

The second level of the Licence To Kill game has Bond on foot shooting it out the army of Sanchez. The game becomes more of a Commando/Who Dares Wins II clone at this point although nowhere near as much fun as those two games. It does though at least freshen the game up and stop the gameplay from becoming too repetitive. You do get another helicopter section after this but this one is different because you are being dangled below the helicopter as Bond (as in the PTS of the film). It's to the credit of the game that they have these different sections but that they all feel part of one overall game rather than completely disjointed (as in the case of Domark's A View To A Kill game).

You also get a plane escape level and a water chase level - which are both passable. The last section of the Licence To Kill game is the tanker chase. If you remember an old arcade game called Spyhunter you'll have a good idea of what to expect from this section. You just race up the screen in a tanker and try and force other trucks off the road. The game is nothing special on the graphics front (though pleasantly colourful) and the over familiarity of this type of game (of which there were billions on the C64) makes the gameplay get old quite fast in certain levels. Mixing up the gameplay with slightly different sorts of sections was therefore very welcome.

The Licence To Kill game is, if my playthrough is anything to go by, quite fiddly and unforgiving on occasion. It might be be that I am simply rubbish at playing this game but it was quite frustrating at times. The lack of originality in the Licence To Kill game is at least compensated for by the variety. The different sections do feel different (a contrast to the Daylights

C64 game where although the backdrops changed the gameplay stayed exactly the same) and it's fun that they've tried to include the big action setpieces from the film.

The makers of the Licence To Kill game were allowed to read some of the script in preparation for their game and they do a reasonable job of capturing the main action scenes of the movie within the constrictive confines of the C64. This game was apparently made to a tight schedule so you can give it some leeway. It's definitely an improvement over the Daylights game but still not what you would call a classic of the C64. Not much of Licence To Kill had been shot when the game started development so the faithful nature of the game in relation to the film is pleasing. The programmers of the game even visited Pinewood Studios and met Cubby Broccoli.

Licence to Kill's game earned a respectable 80% in zzap64 (the most famous British gaming magazine of the era) and was better received than the Daylights game. Neither of the Timothy Dalton films inspired a classic game but the C64 versions of The Living Daylights and Licence To Kill are nostalgic time capsules of that era and modest (if frustrating) fun to explore.

Licence to Kill premiered at the Odeon Leicester Square in London on the 13th of June 1989. Bond fans tend to be divided on Licence To Kill to this day and that was certainly the case with critics in 1989. Time Out praised an intense Dalton for mitigating a formula that had become 'lacklustre' while Richard Corliss in Time Magazine thought that Dalton was already showing signs of being bored by the role! 'The Bond women are pallid mannequins,' wrote Corlis, 'and so is the misused Dalton – a moving target in a Savile Row suit. For every plausible reason, he looks as bored in his second Bond film as Sean Connery did in his sixth.'

Alexander Walker in the Evening Standard complained that the violence in Licence To Kill meant the franchise was turning its back on younger viewers. The Times wrote that Licence To

Kill would herald no great surprises for audiences and suggested that the plot had no ambition. Ian Christie in the Daily Express called the film dull and absurd while Iain Johnstone of The Sunday Times complained that the 'gentleman spy' of old had been replaced by a generic action hero.

The New York Times was more generous and wrote that 'Dalton's glowering presence adds a darker tone' although they did have criticisms. 'Dalton is perfectly at home as an angry Bond and as a romantic lead and as an action hero, but he never seems to blend any two of those qualities at once. He does not seem at ease with all of Bond's lines and to the actor's immense credit he seems least comfortable when M. meets him at Hemingway's house, a Key West tourist attraction and tells him to turn over his gun "I guess it's a farewell to arms" says Mr Dalton not quite cringing. They have to stop writing lines like that for the Dalton Bond or he'll really be full of angst.'

The Los Angeles Times was less picky and gave Licence To kill a glowing review. 'Every once in a while, [the Bond series] pulls in its stomach, pops the gun from its cummerbund, arches its eyebrow and gets off another bull's-eye. The newest, Licence to Kill, is probably one of the five or six best of Bond.' Newsweek called Licence To Kill 'a pure, rousingly entertaining action movie' but also suggested that Timothy Dalton was yet to make the part of James Bond his own. Derek Malcom in The Guardian praised the darker tone of the film but suggested it might have been a lot better if it had been directed by someone with more flair than John Glen.

Roger Ebert enjoyed Licence To Kill more than Daylights and wrote - 'On the basis of this second performance as Bond, Dalton can have the role as long as he enjoys it. He makes an effective Bond - lacking Sean Connery's grace and humor, and Roger Moore's suave self-mockery, but with a lean tension and a toughness that is possibly more contemporary. The major difference between Dalton and the earlier Bonds is that he seems to prefer action to sex. But then so do movie audiences, these days. Licence to Kill is one of the best of the recent Bonds.'

The Globe and Mail was less impressed and wrote - "... they've excised Bond from the Bond flicks; they've turned James into Jimmy, strong and silent and (roll over, Britannia) downright American.' Andrew Pilkington in 007 Magazine was also unimpressed by the film and felt it was too grim. He said he left the press screening feeling bored and disappointed. Pilkington felt that Dalton was too 'theatrical' in Licence To Kill and seemed to have lost the natural quality he displayed in The Living Daylights. Pilkington noted that there seemed to be a strange lack of buzz for Licence To Kill and that fans outside the premiere seemed less numerous than in past years.

Sadly, Licence To Kill struggled in the North American blockbuster box-office summer of 1989 (Batman, Indiana Jones and the Last Crusade, Lethal Weapon 2, Ghostbusters 2, Honey I Shrunk the Kids, Star Trek V etc) and was considered to be a financial disappointment there. It made around $34 million in the United States - which was definitely disappointing because Daylights had made over $50 million in America and a number of films made over $100 million at the North American box-office in the amazing movie summer of 1989. It is said that MGM basically withdrew the marketing for Licence To Kill after a week and one can believe that because the picture plainly struggled to hold its position.

It was definitely an unusual sort of year in 1989 because even films that were not obvious blockbusters like Parenthood and When Harry Met Sally outgrossed Licence To Kill three or four times over in the United States that summer. Licence To Kill's tepid performance in North America was especially galling (and perhaps confusing) for EON because the tougher tone and increased violence was tailored for the American market (where action movies seemed to be becoming more violent all the time). One of the most frustrating things about Licence To Kill's disappointing box-office in North America is that the movie scored high marks with preview audiences in the United States. With a more committed marketing campaign it could (and probably should) have been a much bigger hit.

Let's remember though that Licence To kill did good business around the world even if it didn't completely set the world alight in North America. Licence To Kill made $156.2 million in total, which was respectable but still $40 million down on The Living Daylights. While John Glen felt that Licence to Kill was his best Bond film out of the five he had directed, he later expressed the view that the poor box-office performance of the film in America was a consequence of studio trouble and a confused marketing campaign.

"The thing is that MGM was going through absolute turmoil at that point," said John Glen. "We had, I think, three or four different people on publicity during the course of making it – they were changing every few weeks. So what happened was that they didn't seem to put the effort into selling the picture. If you look at the way they sold Goldeneye, it was a huge campaign, and they did a great job and spent a lot of money on it. They spent a lot of money on Licence to Kill, but it didn't seem to me to be sold as it should have been. I put that down to the fact that the studio was upside-down, heads were changing, people were switching jobs, and new people were coming in all the time. It was a very difficult period."

Amazingly, speculation about Timothy Dalton's future as James Bond began before the dust had even settled on Licence To Kill. The British tabloids ran stories in the summer of 1989 that the studio wanted to replace Dalton with Pierce Brosnan. The shadow of Brosnan increasingly loomed over Timothy Dalton's Bond so heavily that in 1990 a number of people noted that a (soon to be discontinued) cover on John Gardner's latest Bond novel Brokenclaw seemed to illustrate James Bond to look like Pierce Brosnan!

After Brosnan lost out on Bond in 1986, Remington Steele (after two comeback movies in which the lack of enthusiasm by Brosnan was all too apparent) had been swiftly cancelled again - which made NBC's decision to briefly reactivate the show feel all the more petty and pointless. It was fairly obvious that NBC only brought back Remington Steele back because of the publicity and prestige of having the new James Bond actor in one of their shows. Cubby Broccoli however had refused to play this game with NBC.

Brosnan's career was stuttering somewhat circa 1989. The films he had made (Nomads, Taffin, The Deceivers) received poor reviews and he was still struggling to escape from the world of TV miniseries. The one bright spot for Brosnan had been the decent 1987 thriller The Fourth Protocol - in which he did well as a ruthless Russian agent on a secret mission to set off a nuclear device in the West. All in all though, Brosnan would probably have bitten your hand off if you'd offered him James Bond in 1989.

After his initial outbursts at NBC, Pierce Brosnan had shown his class by mostly staying silent about losing out on The Living Daylights. He did this largely out of respect for Timothy Dalton - who he personally knew and also liked. Brosnan did though shoot a 007 inspired Diet Coke commercial in 1988 in which he played a James Bondish Milk Tray Man style character who dodges ninjas and hangs on the side of the train before settling down in a carriage to enjoy a can of coke with a beautiful woman.

The speculation about Dalton's future was obviously a consequence of Licence To Kill not doing nearly as well in the United States as the studio and EON might have hoped. While there might conceivably have been a few MGM executives in 1989 who would have been perfectly happy to put Dalton in the ejector seat and hire Pierce Brosnan, there was zero chance of this actually happening. Dalton was under contract to make a third film and still had the full support of Cubby Broccoli and EON.

Besides, there was no reason to believe that with a better

marketing campaign (and a bit more luck with the box-office competition next time around) a third Dalton film couldn't be a success. It's not as if Timothy Dalton's two Bond films had completely bombed. Both got plenty of positive reviews and turned in a profit. If anything, the prospect of a third Dalton film was rather intriguing now because it would fascinating to see what direction it took.

Cubby Broccoli made some public comments after the dust settled on Licence To Kill where he suggested that Licence was lacking some of the wry humour and fun which audiences had come to expect from James Bond. Dalton's third Bond film then was expected to undergo a slight course correction and be a slightly lighter and more outlandish affair than Licence To Kill. There's no reason why Dalton couldn't have worked in a film that was less 'angry' than Licence To Kill. Dalton had already displayed some charm in the somewhat lighter Living Daylights. It wasn't as if he was only capable of playing a grumpy James Bond intent on killing everyone.

One popular criticism of the Dalton films was that the villains were not in the classic Bond tradition. It is true that they were rather unconventional. Koskov was basically a smooth fast talking conman while Sanchez was a real world sort of villain who might plausibly exist. It was expected then that Dalton's third film would probably have a more over the top fantastical sort of villain. Because Bond films are always set in the present day, the producers and writers often tend to be somewhat pretentious about topical elements and reflecting the real world. While Bond films will sometimes use a news headline for inspiration, they do not really reflect the real world and nor should they do so. We go to see James Bond films to escape from the real world - not to be reminded that the world is a terrible place. One look at the news is all we need for that.

Despite the occasional overblown claim by the producers that Bond must reflect the real world this has never really been the case. We never saw Bond fighting ISIS or battling child traffickers or people smugglers. We never saw Bond fighting in the Falklands War. We never saw him fighting in the Gulf Wars. The topicality of Bond is a superficial sort of gloss that amounts to one of the writers calling Donald Trump a real life Bond villain or Barbara Broccoli saying that in today's climate Bond women can no longer wander around in bikinis with a secret microtape stuffed down their underwear. The Dalton films were grounded by the standards of Bond but they were not radically realistic.

Another criticism of Dalton's Bond that surfaced after Licence To Kill was lack of humour. Humour was the biggest difference between the James Bond books written by Ian Fleming and the James Bond film franchise created by Cubby Broccoli and Harry Saltzman. The films gave Bond (played by the peerless Sean Connery) deadpan quips and witty lines. Humour became an essential part of the franchise. Sean Connery and Roger Moore had impeccable timing when it came to dispensing the trademark Bond quips. These quips sounded less natural though coming from the mouth of Timothy Dalton. Timothy Dalton always seemed to be searching for a subtext in his lines but sometimes a quip is just a quip and didn't have to have any great significance beyond that.

It's not really as if the Dalton era required much of a course correction. Both of his films had a respectable critical reception. Years later, no one suggested Daniel Craig should leave the role after his second film Quantum of Solace proved to be a critical misfire so why should Dalton have had to leave after Licence To Kill? All it probably required was for a third Dalton film to be more like Daylights than Licence To Kill and freshen things up with a new director. A new director was clearly on the cards anyway as Dalton seemed less than enthusiastic at the prospect of working with John Glen again. *

In their overview of Licence To Kill, 007 Magazine suggested that the third Dalton film should be directed by John McTiernan, Richard Donner, or Lewis Gilbert. Although these would clearly have been interesting and talented choices it is probably doubtful that two Hollywood directors as high profile (not to mention expensive) as McTiernan and Donner would have been realistic possibilities. John McTiernan was red hot after Predator and Die Hard and would probably have been too busy anyway. Lewis Gilbert had of course directed You Only Live Twice, The Spy Who Loved Me, and Moonraker for EON. It's highly doubtful they would have gone back to Gilbert (who was knocking on a bit by now) but it's a rather fun thought to think of the director of The Spy Who Loved Me having a stab at a Tim Dalton film! I'd have paid money to watch that.

Nothing too radical was really required for a third Dalton film. If anything it just needed to be a little more conventional. The Bond franchise had faced far bigger headaches in its past and would again in the future. There was the headache of replacing Connery for OHMSS and then the headache of replacing Connery AGAIN after Diamonds Are Forever.

The mediocre reception to The Man with the Golden Gun required something of a course correction back to the extravaganza Bonds of the sixties. The excesses of Moonraker then required a course correction to the more grounded (for Roger Moore at least) For Your Eyes Only. Years later, the creative dead end experienced by Barbara Broccoli and Michael G. Wilson after Die Another Day led to a four year hiatus and a complete reboot of the franchise. Making a third Dalton film was child's play compared to some of these past and future headaches.

* Timothy Dalton is alleged to have requested at the time that his third Bond film should have a new director. A few years later Dalton left the production of Christopher Columbus: The Discovery after John Glen came onboard as director in place of George Pan Cosmatos. In his memoir, John Glen said - "While waiting for his third Bond assignment, Tim had agreed to play Columbus. My arrival, however, seemed to initiate a change of heart and Tim soon decided he didn't want to appear in the film after all. I don't know whether Tim thought that appearing in another John Glen film would typecast him, but I

hope that his departure wasn't entirely due to me. Whatever his reasons, the official story was that Tim had decided not to play Christopher Columbus because of 'creative differences' - whatever that means." It was a lucky escape for Dalton in the end because Christopher Columbus: The Discovery bombed and swept the board at the Golden Raspberries. The failure of the film pretty much ended Glen's career as a movie director and he ended up directing episodes of Gerry Anderson's Space Precinct for television.

CHAPTER TEN

While he waited for his third Bond film to fall into place, Timothy Dalton made The King's Whore (a period drama that never got a US theatrical release) and showed he was unafraid to move away from the Bond persona and image. He then made The Rocketeer - which gave Dalton the chance to show that he could actually be funny. Meanwhile, what of James Bond? In 1989/1990, Alfonse M. Ruggiero Jr, a writer on the TV show Miami vice, sent Michael G. Wilson a treatment of his idea for a Bond film. Wilson deemed that Ruggiero's treatment was of little use because of its similarities to Licence To Kill (Ruggiero's ideas are said to have involved drugs runners in Mexico) but he was impressed enough to suggest that Ruggiero should personally work with him on a story for Bond 17. By May 1990, this Ruggiero/Wilson treatment had been completed.

Behind the scenes, the writer Richard Maibaum and regular director John Glen were told that their services would not be required on Bond 17. Cubby Broccoli, clearly still stung by the disappointing American grosses of Licence To Kill, was intent on shaking things up somewhat in the Bond family before the cameras started rolling again. It was no great surprise that John Glen would not be coming back given that he and Timothy Dalton had a falling out near the end of production on Licence To Kill. It also made sense creatively to make a change in the director's chair at this point. John Glen had been an excellent servant to the Bond series for many years but it was logical to hire someone new to direct the first Bond film of the 1990s. Bond 17 would also be pivotal to Timothy Dalton's era so EON clearly wanted a director who might offer a fresh perspective and style.

Cubby Broccoli would later hire Will Davis and William Osborne (who wrote the Arnold Schwarzenegger film Twins) to provide further drafts of the Ruggiero/Wilson story. Willard Huyck & Gloria Katz (who wrote on films like American

Graffiti, Indiana Jones and the Temple of Doom, and Howard the Duck) were also approached by Broccoli with a view to refining the story. A start date of 1991 was planned and the Canadian director Ted Kotcheff (best known for directing Sly Stallone in First Blood) was the prime candidate to sit in the director's chair.

While he had a reasonable track record when it came to action (not only First Blood but also Uncommon Valor), Kotcheff was not the most exciting choice. His recent films at the time (Switching Channels, Weekend at Bernie's, Winter People) had all been mediocre and didn't really give you much confidence that he'd be a tremendous upgrade on John Glen or the person to shake up the franchise with fresh energy and invention. In a 2017 interview for the Money into Light blog, Kotcheff said he was offered Bond 17 but turned it down because the proposed fee was too low. "It was the only time that I turned down a movie over money. I thought 'If I'm going to do a Bond movie, I want to get paid.' Nobody is going to look at a Bond film and say 'Oh, what a great directorial job.' On a Bond film what you need is a good stunt co-ordinator. It's too bad. I do like the series, and I love Sean Connery in particular."

A more interesting and widely reported candidate to direct Bond 17 was John Landis. Landis was no stranger to EON as he had been one of many writers who pitched ideas for what became The Spy Who Loved Me. At one point, Landis had been one of the hottest film directors in the world thanks to Animal House, An American Werewolf in London, and The Blues Brothers. There was briefly a time when Landis was pure A-list and an equal to the likes of Steven Spielberg. Landis however was forever tarnished by the 1983 anthology film Twilight Zone: The Movie - in which he directed one of the four segments. The movie was something of a dream project for Landis and his friend Steven Spielberg (who was also producing the film and directing a segment himself).

The Twilight Zone film was completely overshadowed by a

horrific helicopter accident on the set which killed actor Vic Morrow and two child extras (Renee Chen and My-ca Dinh Le) during the shooting of the John Landis contribution. Landis and his team had secretly paid the families of the child extras under the table and used the children on a dangerous night shoot (this was all in violation of California's child labour laws). The tragic accident swiftly ended the friendship between Spielberg and Landis and led to a ten year manslaughter case. To the surprise of most observers, Landis somehow managed to evade any serious charges for the accident. Landis had needlessly put his lead actor and two child extras at risk simply because of his determination to capture a great shot for his film.

Landis had Vic Morrow (who was no spring chicken) wade through a wind lashed river carrying the children as huge explosions went off in the background and a helicopter (which Landis allegedly ordered to get lower) hovered above them. Tragically, debris from one of the explosions hit the helicopter's rotor and it flipped over and landed on top of Morrow and the children. Two books were written about the Twilight Zone accident and they both painted John Landis as a bombastic, reckless, and dangerous egomaniac. The career of John Landis never quite recovered from the awful Twilight Zone tragedy. Despite the success he had with Michael Jackson's Thriller video, Landis found his status in Hollywood reduced thanks to the Twilight Zone affair and the poor reception of films like Into the Night and Spies Like Us. He never managed to get back to the Hollywood top table again although he did have a solid box-office hit with the 1988 Eddie Murphy comedy Coming to America.

John Landis would have been the first American to direct a Bond film. He could do action (look at all those car chases in The Blues Brothers!), he could do comedy (even An American Werewolf in London is funny and deadpan), and was an energetic and inventive director. The thought of John Landis (even a Landis past his prime) making a Bond film was a lot more interesting than the prospect of Ted Kotcheff. What would inevitably have complicated any chance of Landis doing a Bond film though was the question of creative control. Landis was the sort of director who wanted the final cut or at least be the person calling all the shots. You can't imagine EON taking a back seat to a big personality like Landis although Michael G. Wilson was said to be genuinely interested in hiring him.

The most offbeat candidate being linked to Bond 17 when it came to the director was later John Byrum. John Byrum was not exactly a household name. He had directed the little seen British film Inserts in the 1970s and later directed Bill Murray in a 1984 adaptation of W. Somerset Maugham's 1944 novel The Razor's Edge. The Razor's Edge didn't make any money and got mixed reviews. Byrum seemed to be working in television by the time his name started to be linked to the Bond franchise. Another candidate was Roger Spottiswoode - who said that he was approached about directing Bond 17 in 1991. Several years later, Spottiswoode would direct Pierce Brosnan's second Bond film Tomorrow Never Dies.

The rumoured title of Bond 17 in the media at the time was Portrait of a Lady. That's not a typo. It really was rumoured early on. Naturally of course that old unused Fleming title The Property of a Lady was then rumoured too - though with no truth. Quantum of Solace (another unused Fleming title) was also thrown into the speculation as a potential title. A title more seriously under active consideration for Dalton's third Bond film though was Goldeneye. Things were definitely happening behind the scenes. The Cannes Film Festival in 1990 featured a banner suggesting Bond would return to screens in 1991.

It is certainly interesting that, despite the mixed reception to Licence To Kill and disappointing North American gross, Cubby Broccoli was intent on a business as usual approach and had no desire for a hiatus or time to stew on of the direction the franchise might go. He was also clearly still 100% behind Timothy Dalton. While all these plans were slowly stirred and simmered though, a storm cloud entered the horizon. MGM/UA was sold to Pathé Communications. Danjaq, the Swiss based parent company of EON, sued MGM/UA and its new chairman to protect the TV distribution rights of the James Bond series from being devalued. These legal wrangles would, unknown to anyone at the time, drag on for much longer than expected and have profound consequences for Bond 17.

The Bond 17 script treatment by Alfonse M. Ruggiero Jr and Michael G Wilson concerned the handover of Hong Kong from Britain to China (which was set to happen in 1997). An accident at a British chemical weapons plant leads to Bond investigating Sir Henry Lee Ching - a British-Chinese entrepreneur. The story takes place in Hong Kong, Japan, and China, and has Bond teaming up with a female master thief and part-time CIA agent named Connie Webb. Now that the Cold War was apparently no more, the Bond team obviously looked to China (as the remaining communist superpower at the time after the fall of the Soviet union) for inspiration when it came to intrigue and villains.

The synopsis for the script treatment went like this - 'A mysterious explosion devastates a Scottish chemical weapons factory. The perpetrator of this misdeed already announces other attacks and 007 is sent to the Far East to investigate a thief, Connie Webb, who may well have a connection with all this. Very quickly, Bond realises that Sir Henry Lee Ching, a Hong Kong businessman working in high technology, is not the man as respectable as one might think. 007 will have to team up with the Chinese secret services in order to discover the plans of the mysterious Henry Lee Ching, and prevent a global disorder that could lead to the Third World War...'

Ruggiero's ideas were obviously based on the lucrative arms trade. The wealthy Western nations sell a lot of weapons and military technology around the world - sometimes to governments or regimes you wouldn't exactly describe as ethical. Ruggiero came up with the idea of having the villain be a manufacturer of military technology who is secretly using his own technology to gain control of weapons systems and missiles. It should be noted that in the world of James Bond this is hardly an original idea. Ian Fleming's 1955 novel Moonraker had already done a similar plot. Fleming's story is about an enigmatic tycoon called Sir Hugo Drax. Drax is developing a nuclear missile system for Britain known as the Moonraker project. It is only Drax though who has total control of the missile.

The most interesting thing about the Alfonse M. Ruggiero Jr and Michael G Wilson script treatment is that the villain is an expert in robotics and computers and threatens to paralyse all military computer systems around the world. "Fools believe that their weapons make them invincible," he boasts. "In their paranoid whims, they waste billions on weapons systems built by my companies, but in reality they have become imprisoned from their own armor. All military and commercial units in the world can be instantly paralyzed from this room!" The microchip entrepreneur Ching was set to be a much more 'old school' and fantastical villain than we'd seen so far in the Timothy Dalton era.

Henry Lee Ching, we learn in the treatment, has become very powerful and is buying companies left, right, and centre all around the world. He's like the Jeff Bezos of his day. It turns out that Ching's father fled China to Burma years ago where he became a brutal warlord and drugs baron. Quen Low, one of the Chinese agents that James Bond works with in the story, says that Ching's father and his men were wiped out by Chinese and Burmese authorities but that his son and wife managed to flee to Hong Kong.

Henry Lee Ching has understandably always tried to hide the shameful past of his family. Ching built a financial empire thanks to his genius with electronics but he is bent on revenge against China for what they did to his father. Ching has supplied military equipment and technology to Britain - which would explain how he got a knighthood. Gustav Graves in Die

Another Day seems to owe something to Ching but it could be that Graves - like Ching - simply owes something to Hugo Drax!

The PTS of Bond 17 in the Ruggiero/Wilson treatment was potentially set to be a spectacular sequence where a Scottish chemical weapons facility is destroyed when one of the robotic machines there begins to malfunction and go berserk. It is equally possible that this sequence might have been used after the titles though. Although all the scenes of robotics in the film sounds far-fetched, EON were deadly serious and even hired Disney's Imagineering department to come up with some designs. There patently was a clear desire to inject more fantasy (and even a little sci-fi) into the Dalton era. We should remember that EON were not planning to make James Bond vs The Terminator. The robots were inspired by real industrial machines.

In the treatment by Alfonse M. Ruggiero Jr and Michael G Wilson, Sir Henry Lee Ching arranges various accidents at military facilities around the world - which naturally keeps James Bond busy. Ching is described as a young and handsome villain who is indifferent to the human race and only cares about science. The climax was set to feature a fight between Bond and Ching in which Bond gets the upper hand by using a blowtorch. Bond was also set to work with a veteran spy named Denholm Crisp in the story. Other characters included a Chinese intelligence operative named Mi Wai and an assassin named Rodin who has numerous high technology gadgets - including a Predator style thermal imaging vision system inside his motorcycle helmet.

Bond fans will note that a number of ideas and themes in the Ruggiero/Wilson script (like the Far East setting, tension over Hong Kong, a plot to engineer a conflict between China and the West, and the female Chinese agent character) were later recycled and used in Tomorrow Never Dies. Highlights of the Bond 17 script treatment include an explosion in the Nanking Atomic Plant, a skiing/avalanche sequence (Connie Webb is revealed to be a former skier who would have gone to the Olympics were it not for an injury and we know that Bond is an expert skier too) which ended up in The World Is Not Enough, and a car chase between the Aston Martin and Rodin's high-tech computer car (this sequence ends with Bond using an ejector seat and parachute to escape).

During the sequence where Rodin duels with Bond in his high-tech car, Ching watches the action with the captured Connie on a giant viewscreen as if it is a computer game. The big chase which pits Bond's DB5 against Rodin's high-tech supercar predates the high-tech car showdown in Die Another Day. This sequence is fun because Bond's Aston Martin has plenty of gadgets and tricks of its own to pit against the lethally technological vehicle of Rodin. There is also a sequence where Bond is tied up and tasered, superconductivity intrigue, a Lamborghini chase, a battle with twin Japanese villains named the Kohoni brothers (the Kohoni twin brothers are leaders of the Kohoni industrial empire), and a climax in the sewers of Hong Kong. 007 also has to foil a missile strike on Shanghai and flood Sir Henry Ching's space-age command HQ.

An important character in the treatment is Nigel Yupland - a Ministry of Defence hotshot who wants to dismantle the Double-O-Section now that Cold War has thawed. This character has some obvious similarities with Denbigh in the Sam Mendes film Spectre. Yupland has the ear of the Prime Minster and there is a scene in the treatment which takes place in the House of Commons. While 007 is able to deduce that Ching is a villain he finds it difficult to persuade Yupland. Yupland travels to Hong Kong to try and take over the investigation that Bond is supposed to be conducting.

The DB5 also returns in the Ruggiero/Wilson treatment. In the script there is only one classic DB5 left in Q branch and Q arranges to have it sent to Bond in the field before the bureaucrats can close down the Double-O section. This treatment provides an expanded role for Q in the same fashion as Licence To Kill did. Q makes a personal visit to Hong Kong to deliver the DB5 to Bond (and of course implores Bond to take good care of the car). There's a great scene Bond drives the DB5 through Hong Kong's colourful new Year celebrations. The treatment also features alpine scenes involving a helicopter which obviously evoke memories of On Her Majesty's Secret Service. Some of the scenes where Bond and Connie ski are also very OHMSS.

There isn't too much detail about the robotic devices in the treatment. This aspect was obviously going to be designed and worked out later. A superconductivity cube in the story is a sort of McGuffin to drive the plot along (in that the characters are all greatly interested in this object). This treatment is much more technology and gadget driven than the two Timothy Dalton films we did get. The villain has a HQ that is described as like a top secret NATO briefing room. This all feels much more like the sort of villain we would get in the Roger Moore films than the villains of Daylights or Licence To Kill. There are a lot of things blowing up in the treatment so explosions and action is not in short supply.

One thing that does feel dated in the treatment is the corporate intrigue and danger having a heavy Japanese element. It was very in vogue in early nineties Hollywood movies to present Japan as a sinister and alien economic threat. The obvious flaws in the script are a heavy sense of deja vu. A microchip businessman as the villain is too similar to A View To A kill and Connie Webb's CIA agent character feels an awful lot like a rehash of Pam Bouvier from Licence To Kill. Yupland eventually orders that Bond should be be taken off the case and be sent back to London but Bond ignores his orders and goes AWOL. This is a lazy moment in the treatment because it is simply repeating the same scenario (Bond goes rogue) we saw in Licence To Kill.

The Alfonse M. Ruggiero Jr and Michael G Wilson treatment has a theme where Bond's relevance is starting to be questioned now that the Cold War is over. Yupland thinks that Bond is an anachronistic cowboy. This theme (of becoming a relic of another time) would be present in 1995's Goldeneye (which unknown to anyone at the time turned out to be the next Bond film that did go into production). Goldeneye, because of both changing times and Barbara Broccoli's increased influence, would even question whether Bond was a sexist dinosaur. You don't get that in this Bond 17 treatment but the germ of this concept is apparent.

You could almost construe this theme of 007's place in the world as a meta commentary by the Bond team on their own franchise. The Soviet Union has collapsed and the 1990s are upon them. They were obviously mulling over such events and trying to work out how much Bond has to change to reflect the times. One other interesting feature of this Bond 17 draft is that Bond is presumed dead at one point and tries to use this to his advantage. Skyfall had a similar concept many years later.

As for whether or not the Ruggiero/Wilson script would have made a good James Bond film, this is a question that seems to sharply divide Bond fans. It had the potential to be very entertaining and fun in the right hands but some Bond fans feel it might be for the best that it never happened and that it (if executed poorly) could have been Timothy Dalton's Die Another Day. The treatment seemed to represent a tonal shift from the two Dalton films to more of an escapist and fantastical sort of Bond film.

The Ruggiero/Wilson treatment seems to be a reaction to criticisms that Licence To Kill was too dark and 'real world' in its plot and villain. The Ruggiero/Wilson treatment is designed to explore the possibility of making Dalton's third film a techno thriller. The blueprint is patently to make 007 more cutting edge and modern for the 1990s. At the time, people really were starting to wonder if the Bond series needed a change of direction. Writing in Starburst after Licence To Kill came out, John Brosnan said that Licence To Kill felt old-fashioned and behind the times in an action landscape of Die Hard and Lethal Weapon.

The Bond 17 treatment seemed to acknowledge this and even included some Die Hard inspired sequences like an attack on a high-tech office and runaway elevator antics. Perhaps the key question is not whether the treatment would have made a passable Bond film but whether or not it would have made a good Timothy Dalton Bond film. It would have been wonderful to have a solid third Dalton film which established him in the role (and did good numbers at the box-office) but it would have been less than wonderful to see his tenure tarnished by a third film that was too silly and didn't suit his portrayal of the character.

We simply don't know how this film would have turned out if it had gone ahead. The treatment would obviously have been extensively refined and changed before it hit the screen. If this treatment had been expanded into a competent screenplay and been given to the right director it probably could have worked. Besides, who wouldn't have wanted to see Timothy Dalton's Bond in Hong Kong battling the technology obsessed henchman Rodin?

CHAPTER ELEVEN

In 1991, Timothy Dalton was back on the big screen in The Rocketeer This is a vastly unappreciated and beautiful looking Joe Johnston Disney film inspired by characters invented by the artist and writer Dave Stevens. The film is set in 1938 and concerns Cliff Secord (Bill Campbell) - a stunt pilot who winds up finding a jet pack which allows him to fly. The jet pack is an invention of Howard Hughes (Terry O'Quinn) but it lands Cliff into all sorts of trouble because mobsters and the Nazis want to get their hands on it.

The Rocketeer was a box-office flop but now (happily) has a cultish following. It's in the tradition of the Indiana Jones series and has a fun backdrop of 30s Hollywood, zeppelins, and Nazi intrigue. There is also a fantastic James Horner score. Jennifer Connelly is memorable as Cliff's actress girlfriend Jenny Blake and Dalton has fun as

Neville Sinclair - a movie star clearly based on Errol Flynn. Sinclair turns out to be a Nazi agent and so Dalton got to do a rather enjoyable turn as a villain.

Dalton, with his background in theatre and costume dramas, is patently enjoying the chance to ham it up when Sinclair is making a movie called The Laughing Bandit. Dalton is not only funny in The Rocketeer but also charismatic. And yet these are two qualities critics of his Bond say he didn't possess as an actor! Timothy Dalton looked terrific in The Rocketeer and it's a great shame that he couldn't make a Bond film at this time. In an appearance on The Arsenio Hall Show to promote The Rocketeer, Dalton said he was still very eager to make another Bond film and that they would have shot one in 1990 were it not for the litigation.

It was decided in the end, with the litigation and legal wrangles frustratingly lingering on and acting as a handbrake to any attempt to fast track Bond 17, to refine the

Ruggiero/Wilson script. Will Davis and William Osborne were next up when it came to writing duties on Bond 17 and made a number of changes (although this draft still featured robotics and the character of Connie Webb). The new script had the villain now named Sir Henry Ferguson. This baddie is not a microchip entrepreneur but the designer of a super advanced plane called the Scimitar.

There was still a Chinese element to the new script as this super advanced plane threatened the West with missiles - all of which naturally had to be foiled by Bond. The story still took place in China and Hong Kong but other locations now included Libya and Las Vegas. Action set-pieces included a car chase in Las Vegas and a finale at the Hoover Dam. The Will Davis and William Osborne script also included a rather eccentric sequence where Bond goes undercover as a cowboy at a rodeo! The Will Davis and William Osborne script is generally deemed to be somewhat more comedic and Roger Moorish at times than the Ruggiero/Wilson draft.

Perhaps the daftest element to the Bond 17 drafts at this point was that the villain's girlfriend was going to be revealed to be a cyborg! It's hard to believe this would have survived had the cameras actually rolled on any version of Bond 17's story drafts. The most interesting thing about the last draft is that it included a theme where Bond was starting to feel his age and wonder if he was still relevant. This is a theme that Sam Mendes would later have in Skyfall. Will Davis and William Osborne said that when it came to any mildly radical ideas or departure from the Bond formula it was Cubby Broccoli who was most resistant to change.

William Davies said that they actually had talks with Timothy Dalton about the script and told him of their idea that Bond was starting to feel his age. Davies said though that Michael G. Wilson felt they never quite managed to nail the story sufficiently for EON move ahead with any of the drafts. Will Davis and William Osborne said they worked on Bond 17 for about a year and did three script treatments.

Casting tittle tattle around this time suggested that Anthony Hopkins (who was still a friend of Dalton - they both made their film debut in Lion in Winter) was interested in playing the villain. Whoopi Goldberg was also linked to the part of a (presumably different) villain in Bond 17 in the press. The speculation concerning Whoopi Goldberg was because she had appeared on a chat show with Timothy Dalton and joked about being in the next Bond film. It seems doubtful that she was really up for a part in the film.

Ken Watanabe was also alleged to be up for a part in the next Bond film, as was John Lone. Sandra Bullock (not yet a big star at the time) was rumoured to be in EON's sights when it came to Bond Girls. Bond 17 got advanced enough at one point to include some location scouting. It is believed that because the Chinese government proved difficult to deal with, EON were looking at locations in Canada and Australia that that could pass for China and Hong Kong respectively. "We had the script," said Timothy Dalton years later. "They were interviewing directors. We were really rolling forward, ready to start. It was actually quite a good story, I thought."

Matters were still complicated though by the litigation. A new Bond film could not go ahead until this was solved. There are conflicting accounts of whether or not Timothy Dalton was still under contract at this point. Some stories have suggested that Dalton's contract to EON ended in 1990 but this doesn't make much sense because Licence To Kill only came out the previous year. It doesn't sound much like Cubby Broccoli to make one-off films with someone he doesn't have signed to any sort of contract! It seems more believable that, as has been stated in other stories, Dalton was still under contract - at least into the early nineties.

You can bet your life that if the litigation hadn't occurred then Cubby Broccoli would have delivered the next Bond film to cinemas in 1991 ot 1992. One of the reasons why Bond films do not arrive on a regular basis anymore is that Barbara Broccoli likes to take on other projects. She has produced films outside the Bond franchise and has even produced plays for Daniel Craig. Her father Cubby, especially when he became the sole Bond producer after Harry Saltzman sold his stake in the franchise, was happy to simply make Bond films and usually had one out every two years. Barbara is more of a 'luvvie' than her father. You have the impression that Barbara dreams of the Bond films winning BAFTAS and Oscars whereas Cubby was simply happy to give fans a couple of hours of undemanding fun in the cinema every few years.

As production on Bond 17 continued to wait for the elusive green light, Timothy Dalton went back to work. The interesting British TV miniseries Framed saw Dalton play against his Bond image again with another morally dubious character, here alongside a young David Morrissey. Dalton also appeared in a 1992 episode of the excellent HBO horror anthology series Tales from the Crypt called Werewolf Concerto. The episode also featured Bond veteran Walter Gotell. Dalton seems to be having fun in Werewolf Concerto although he was rather dismissive of the episode in an interview about his career years later. Dalton said Werewolf Concerto wasn't especially fufilling.

In 1992, the newspapers were full of unlikely stories that the Hollywood producer Joel Silver was planning to buy the James Bond franchise and replace Timothy Dalton with Mel Gibson. In the midst of the litigation wrangles it was reported that Cubby Broccoli put his Bond rights up for sale and Silver was one of the interested parties. However, this sale obviously did not go ahead. Broccoli either never planned to sell in the first place, withdrew his offer, or was simply using the threat of a sale as a tactic in his battle with former MGM/UA owner Kirk Kerkorian and MGM's Giancarlo Parretti - an Italian financier who purchased MGM for $1.2 billion in 1990. Parretti was accused of looting the legendary studio, defaulting on the loan payments to Credit Lyonnais, and bringing the studio to near bankruptcy. Less than a year later, Parretti was forced to resign as Chairman and CEO of MGM.

There was more strange speculation around this time when it was reported in the media that a James Bond television show was in the works and that Robert Powell and Lewis Collins were among the actors who had been approached to play James Bond in this proposed show. To the surprise of absolutely no one, these stories turned out to have no basis in fact. Even so, EON took the step of publishing a statement (more of a warning really) in Variety reminding any 'interested parties' that only they (EON) had the legal rights to make films or television shows based on James Bond.

Behind the scenes, in the middle of the litigation quagmire, Cubby Broccoli asked Timothy Dalton what his thoughts were regarding Bond 17. Dalton told Broccoli that he honestly couldn't see himself returning if his contract was eroded by the endless delays. "Because of the lawsuit, I was free of the contract," said Dalton. "And Mr Broccoli, who I really respected as a producer and as a friend, asked me what I was going to do when it was resolved. I said, 'Look, in all honesty, I don't think that I will continue.' He asked me for my support during that time, which of course, I gave him."

This decision was not set in stone though and Dalton later indicated to Broccoli that he WOULD be interested in returning. This change of heart was in danger of becoming irrelevant though thanks to changes behind the scenes at MGM. John Calley (who was appointed president by the new chairman Frank Mancuso) would eventually take over at MGM and was described as more 'Bond friendly' (in that he was much easier to work with and wanted the cameras rolling on Bond 17 as fast as possible) than his infamous predecessor. The litigation dispute was finally resolved in December 1992.

Variety reported on the welcome end of the tiresome litigation by writing - 'Metro-Goldwyn-Mayer Inc. and Danjaq Inc., producer of the 'James Bond 007' films, said Wednesday they have settled their legal disputes over MGM's right to market and license the Bond films. The settlement could open the way for Danjac to produce and MGM to release another James Bond movie. MGM has been trying to build up its film slate since last spring when it won control of the studio from Italian financier Giancarlo Parretti. The last Bond film, Licence to Kill, was released in 1989. It starred Timothy Dalton as Bond, previously played by Sean Connery and Roger Moore.

'The companies said the agreement settles the suit Danjaq filed in February 1991 against MGM and its former parent company, Pathe Communications Corp. Danjaq claimed in the suit that then-MGM owner Parretti had breached contracts with it by selling the rights to the Bond films to help finance his $1.4 billion purchase of the studio in late 1990 from Kirk Kerkorian. Danjaq originally filed suit against MGM and Pathe in federal court in Los Angeles in October 1990, but that suit was thrown out for being filed in the wrong jurisdiction. Danjaq then filed the suit in state court. Terms of the settlement were not disclosed Wednesday.

"Now that this situation is amicably resolved, we look forward to continuing the rewarding, long-term relationship with Danjaq that MGM and United Artists have historically enjoyed through the Bond and other films,' said Alan Ladd Jr., MGM's co-chairman and co-chief executive officer. 'I am delighted this legal obstacle has been removed and I hope to be able to announce exciting new production plans in the near future,' said Albert R. Broccoli, chairman of Danjaq. Danjaq owns the exclusive rights to produce feature films and television series based on the character James Bond, created by British novelist Ian Fleming. Beginning with 'Dr. No' in 1962, Danjaq has produced 16 Bond films. Most of the films were released through United Artists, which MGM acquired in the early 1980s.

'The companies said the settlement does not affect Danjaq claims against Kerkorian, Kerkorian's Tracinda Corp. and former MGM executive Jeffrey Barbakow. MGM and its owner Credit Lyonnais Bank Nederland N.V. filed lawsuits earlier this week against Kerkorian, alleging the billionaire suckered the bank when he sold off the studio two years ago to Parretti. The suits seek at least $1.5 billion in damages. The bank, which provided financing for the deal and wound up owning the studio, is seeking no less than $500 million in damages, while MGM is asking for at least $750 million in damages. Also named as defendants in the suits were Tracinda and Barbakow, along with former executive Stephen Silbert and Houlihan Lokey, Howard & Zukin Inc., the investment bankers who provided the fairness opinion on the deal.'

John Calley was eager to get Bond 17 into production. However, Calley was most definitely not eager to see Timothy Dalton back as Bond. Calley didn't believe that Timothy Dalton was much of a draw and wanted a more bankable leading man to play 007. Calley's thinking was sadly predictable and seemed to forget that James Bond is the star - not the actor who plays him. When a new Bond film comes out now, no one goes to the cinema to watch the new Daniel Craig film. They are going to watch the new James Bond film. The same can be said of all the Bond actors. No one who went to see Die Another Day or Goldeneye were heading out to watch the new Pierce Brosnan film. They were off to see the new Bond film.

The Brosnan and Craig films did well at the box-office but neither Brosnan nor Craig was a star nor a box-office attraction when they landed the role. And while their Bond films sold plenty of tickets, Pierce Brosnan and Daniel Craig also appeared in a number of films outside the Bond franchise that hardly anyone went to see. The Brosnan and Craig films did much better than Licence To Kill because they had gargantuan highly professional marketing campaigns and were released in the Winter when there was far less competition at the box-office. Licence To Kill enjoyed none of these advantages.

The Bond franchise is one of the few examples of a huge mainstream movie where it doesn't really matter who the leading man is. No one knew Sean Connery from Adam when he was cast as Bond. Daniel Craig was hardly a household name when he got the part. Pierce Brosnan was making television movies when he was cast as Bond. The only actor who had a reasonably high profile going into Bond was Roger Moore - thanks to his television shows The Saint and The Persuaders. Roger was most definitely not a film star though at the time and had no track record to speak of when it came to opening a movie with his mere presence.

The biggest problem facing Bond 17 was not the leading man. The biggest problem with Bond 17 was the usual checklist of concerns that face any new James Bond film. Coming up with new stunts. Keeping up with the action movie rivals. Coming up with a vaguely topical plot. Keeping Bond relevant. Finding a good script. Casting good actors. Finding interesting new locations. Coming up with new gadgets. And (crucially in the case of Bond 17) making sure the marketing campaign and release date affords the film every advantage possible when it hits the cinemas. These were the prime concerns of Bond 17 and any Bond film you care to mention.

It was reported in the press that John Calley had suggested four names to EON who MGM would find acceptable as James Bond in Bond 17. These names were alleged to be Hugh Grant, Ralph Fiennes, Liam Neeson, and Pierce Brosnan. EON however dug their heels in and insisted that it was up to Timothy Dalton if he wanted to come back. They did not want to be disloyal to Dalton and replace him with another actor. Besides, they thought Dalton was an excellent Bond and deserved a chance to cement his legacy with a third film.

CHAPTER TWELVE

EON seemed to lose interest in the existing Bond 17 drafts at some point (despite a 'polish' by Willard Huyck & Gloria Katz) and another potential third Dalton script soon appeared on the horizon. John Calley liked the idea of the team behind the 1993 hit Cliffhanger working on Bond 17. Cliffhanger was an entertaining Sly Stallone action film best described as Die Hard on a mountain range. Calley felt that Cliffhanger's Finnish director Renny Harlin would be perfect to bring Bond into the 1990s. The elaborate plane heist section near the beginning of Cliffhanger involving Qualen's gang is just a little too long perhaps but serves as an impressive aerial set-piece (inspiring a similar scene in a Harrison Ford film called Air Force One) and is the type of grand scale villain caper you wish the James Bond series still bothered to do.

Renny Harlin had recently directed Die Hard 2 (a competent if mechanical sequel to the classic original) and was very good at action scenes. Harlin was approached about Bond 17 but did not like the fact that EON were still planning to use Timothy Dalton again. "Actually, to be honest," he later said, "what happened at that point was I was interested in doing the Bond movie, but there was an actor in it that I didn't believe in. And I'm not going to say that his name is Timothy Dalton. I just didn't think that he made a good Bond. I said that you had to recast and come up with a new actor for it. And they refused and said 'he's great', and I was like 'he is not James Bond'. So that was why I walked away from that job."

Harlin was definitely out of the picture but Cliffhanger's writer Michael France was hired to work on a brand new Bond 17 script that would have nothing to do with existing drafts. France said that it was no picnic getting the Bond gig. Around thirty other writers were in contention and his agent had to lobby hard on his behalf. After meetings with Barbara Broccoli and Michael G. Wilson to pitch his ideas, it was arranged for Michael France to go and visit Cubby Broccoli. Everyone at

EON was impressed enough by France to approve hiring him. The name of the Bond 17 script that France began work on was Goldeneye.

Variety reported that Bond 17 had a budget of $40 million and would be 'put on the fast track' when the script by Michael France was ready. Michael Caton-Jones (the director of Memphis Belle, Scandal, and Doc Hollywood) was said by Variety to be in negotiations to direct the new Bond film. Variety noted though that it was uncertain who would play James Bond in the film. They reported that Timothy Dalton had met with producers Barbara Broccoli and Michael G. Wilson (by now, Cubby Broccoli was suffering from heart trouble and taking more of a back seat) but no final decision regarding Dalton's future had been made.

In the August 1993 edition of Film review there was an update on Bond and EON were quoted as saying that no decision had been made yet but that they were hopeful of Timothy Dalton coming back. In 1993, Dalton gave an interview to The Daily Mail and (when asked about James Bond) said that Michael France was working on a script and that production would start in 1994. It is fairly clear then the film which eventually became Goldeneye was, at its inception at least, written for Timothy Dalton.

Michael France's script had an interesting concept at its heart which managed to survive various revisions by later writers and remain in the actual film. France's big idea was to have another Double O agent in the story. "It occurred to me," said France, "that we`d never really seen Bond interacting with another Double O sector agent. In the rest of the series, they are nameless, faceless characters. M says, '003 got killed in Malaysia but he sent us this expository note', or something, and the story would move on with just a slight reaction from Bond, if any at all. That seemed false to me. I thought Bond would have very good friends in the sector - that they`d be as tight as men who go into combat together -- and I thought it would really be something to build up that kind of relationship and make a Double O agent the villain."

The script by Michael France was set in post-Soviet Russia and revolved around Augustus Trevelyan - a former Double O agent who was a mentor to Bond. Trevelyan betrayed MI6 and defected to the Soviet Union during the Cold War. His actions caused the death of two British agents so Bond is sent on a personal revenge mission. Trevelyan seeks to control an EMP satellite weapon and Bond naturally has to foil these plans. While you can clearly detect the bare bones of what would become Goldeneye in France's script there are a number of differences between this early draft and what we actually got on the big screen in 1995. Trevelyan is a much older character in France's script than the more youthful Trevelyan portrayed by Sean Bean in the movie.

The Bond producers had Anthony Hopkins in mind for the part of Augustus Trevelyan. Several years later they unsuccessfully tried top get Hopkins to play Carver in Tomorrow Never Dies. The early version of Goldeneye by Michael France was literally wall to wall action at times. In fact, so festooned with action was France's draft that EON later took out several action scenes and 'banked' them to use in later films (much to the public irritation of France). The most obvious example is the scene in The World Is Not Enough where the helicopters attack with buzzsaws chained underneath. This sequence was in Michael France's Goldeneye draft. The buzzsaw scenes are so similar that they had to give France a writing credit on The World Is Not Enough.

The Michael France script begins with a PTS action sequence involving a futuristic train. It also featured General Pushkin from The Living Daylights and the M in France's script is clearly still Robert Brown. France had Xenia using pressure points (as opposed to her thighs) to kill victims and Trevelyan plans to destroy New York rather than London in this first Goldeneye draft. The basic structure of what would become the 1995 film Goldeneye is very apparent - though changes would of course be made in the months to come.

Michael France was not the only writer developing potential story ideas for Bond 17. Variety reported at this time that - 'Danjaq Inc. has hired Richard Smith and John Cork to pen separate scripts for Agent 007, raising to three the James Bond movies in development. The news comes barely two weeks after MGM/United Artists co-chairman/co-CEO Alan Ladd Jr. confirmed that UA is back in the Bond business with Danjaq producers Albert R. (Cubby) Broccoli, his daughter Barbara and stepson Michael G. Wilson, after a four-year hiatus. Cliffhanger co-script Michael France is now penning 17th in the series. He has not been pitted in a script race with Smith or Cork, Danjaq spokesman Charles Juroe told Daily Variety. "There is no question about it: France is writing Bond 17. These other two gentlemen are writing for future Bonds down the line, assuming (the revived series is) a success," said Juroe, who has worked in one capacity or another on all 16 Bond films.

'Juroe is back in action himself after having retired when a flurry of (now settled) lawsuits made Licence to Kill the last Bond pic in 1989. Bond veteran said until the lawsuits ground things to a halt, having one or two Bond scripts was routine for a company used to producing a sequel every other year. "When you get up to 17 in one series, you do things differently. You don't wait until 17 is a success to say, 'Oh, we better do another one,' "Juroe quipped. "This two-year cycle does not give Danjaq the luxury to wait 10 or 11 months down the line to get started on the next one. They've learned they have to be ahead of the game. When United Artists say they're ready to do another one, they're expected to have one ready."

'And now that the series is back on track, it's no surprise the two new writers are keeping their synopses top secret. Cork, the scriptwriter of the Whoopi Goldberg/Sissy Spacek period melodrama The Long Walk Home, impressed the Broccolis with his idea, Juroe said. Smith has a diverse list of credits that includes everything from acting (Fathers of Pop), producing (TV movie Blackout) and makeup (Life Force).

However, his first professional screenplay was the Sylvester Stallone starrer Lock Up, a credit he shared with Jeb Stuart and Henry Rosenbaum. Juroe figures the two new writers will fit right into the Bond beat at the Broccoli camp. "When we were in our two-year cycle... there was a great deal of scriptwriting going on, based on Ian Fleming's books. After 'Live and Let Die,' sometimes it would just be the title. For instance, 'The Living Daylights' first script was only 27 pages. Fleming wrote it as a short story, "which was later adapted by the team of Richard Maibaum and Michael G. Wilson. And are they writing for thesp Timothy Dalton? "Dalton is the Bond of record," Juroe said.'

A 37 page story treatment for Bond 17 titled Reunion in Death was delivered by Richard Smith near the end of 1993. Reunion in Death was heavily inspired by the Ian Fleming novel You Only Live Twice. Fleming's You Only Live Twice takes place after the shattering events of On Her Majesty's Secret Service. The synopsis for Fleming's novel is - 'Shattered by the murder of his wife at the hands of Ernst Stavro Blofeld, James Bond has gone to pieces as an agent. M gives him one last chance, sending him to Japan for a near-impossible mission. There Bond is trained in the fighting arts of Ninja warriors and sent to infiltrate a mysterious fortress known as the 'Castle of Death' - a place of nightmares where a lethal poisoned garden destroys all who go there - and awakens an old, terrifying enemy. You Only Live Twice sees Bond's final encounter with an insane mastermind - one that could mean the end for 007...'

The story in Richard Smith's Reunion in Death has Bond in Japan investigating Yasuhiro Nakasone - an industrialist connected to the Yakuza. Nakasone's wife Michiko serves as one of Bond's allies though. The plot of Reunion with Death revolves around the murder of Sir Robert Grey - a friend of M. It was of course Nakasone who was behind the murder because of his desire to control the world's microchip market. Interestingly, Bond's secretary Loelia Ponsonby is a character in Reunion in Death. The treatment begins with Bond killing an agent in a skyscraper. The skyscraper PTS in Reunion in Death ends with Bond parachuting from the building.

The character of Sir Robert Grey in Reunion with Death is the boss of a company that produces highly advanced technology. However, because of a bad accident at one of their Far East plants, financial woes lead to them having to consider selling their scientific research department to a Japanese company. Bond, M, and Grey are meeting at a building in London when the building is struck by a missile. Bond manages to save M but Grey is killed in the attack. Bond learns that a group in Malaysia is claiming responsibility for the attack on Grey in revenge for the accident at Grey's Malaysia plant costing many lives.

James Bond is given permission to go to Italy to investigate because three missiles of the kind used in the London attack were recently stolen from a military base in Rome. A fairly lengthy Italian section is part of the treatment. Bond discovers that a man named Dante might have been responsible for the missile theft and so seduces Dante's mistress to get information. 007 must work with an Italian MI6 contact in this part of the story. There's a sequence where Bond and his contact go to a Verdi opera and the contact is killed - leading to Bond chasing a Chinese henchman through underground tunnels. This opera sequence appears to have been an influence on an opera sequence in the 2008 Daniel Craig film Quantum of Solace.

In Richard Smith's treatment, M is injured in hospital because of the London attack. James Bond is given a new temporary boss but he doesn't get on with him very well. The new M even tries to close the investigation into Grey's death and take 007 off the case. Bond continues to secretly consult the injured M (the real M you might say!) in hospital. This is a nice touch and shows that Bond has loyalty and even some affection for M. You could imagine these scenes working quite well with Timothy Dalton and Robert Brown.

Bond then goes to meet a man named Byron Banning. Banning inherited Grey's industrial empire and has received a letter inviting him to a meeting concerning the sale of the scientific research wing of the company. The letter is cryptic and vaguely menacing. James Bond decides that he should pose as the company man representing Banning at this meeting. 007 goes to Japan where he is met by Ryuichi Tanaka (Tiger Tanaka's son). The company with interests in Grey's business empire is called Asahi. The owner of this company is Yasuhiro Nakasone. 007 learns that Yasuhiro Nakasone is heavily involved in the Yakuza (which is sort of like Japan's version of the Mafia).

The meeting takes place at a grand party event full of geishas and samurai imagery. Bond is met by Nakasone's lawyer for the proposed business transaction but insists on meeting with Nakasone personally. Nakasone arrives with his wife Michiko and is irritated when Bond introduces himself to Michiko without asking permission. Bond refuses to sign a business contract (much to Nakasone's annoyance) and so is invited to meet Nakasone again in the Japanese mountains. Meanwhile, there is some intrigue when Bond discovers that Nakasone has him under surveillance and is watching his every move. There is then a chase scene where Bond deduces he is being followed in the city. 007 ends up killing his antagonist in a sauna.

Nakasone has a very Flemingesque medieval castle in the mountains which has a samurai theme. Bond travels to the castle and meets Michiko. She is impressed that Bond can speak Japanese and they both find they have Oxbridge in common. Smith's script makes it clear that Michiko is unhappy in her marriage. Nakasone arrives and is immediately suspicious that his wife is becoming too familiar with Bond. At dinner, Bond deliberately irritates Nakasone by talking directly to Michiko. A type of fish is served which can be deadly and poisonous if not prepared correctly. Bond impresses Nakasone by eating this fish with no trepidation.

Michiko later meets Bond alone and they kiss. She tells Bond that her husband was responsible for Grey's death and she also reveals herself to be a secret contact named 'Dragon' who has been sending messages. Michiko wants revenge on her husband because he was responsible for the death of her father. Bond and Michiko are being watched though and when 007 tries to leave by helicopter he is given sleeping gas and captured by Nakasone's henchman. Bond wakes up tied to a chair and is interrogated by Nakasone. His henchman Ng breaks two of Bond's fingers (an idea taken from Fleming's novel Live and Let Die).

Michiko comes to Bond's rescue and helps him escape. 007 uses a boat under the castle to flee and a huge chase ensues. This chase goes on for some time (with Bond pursued by helicopters) and 007 eventually ends up Seagaia Ocean Dome (which used to be one of the largest indoor water parks in the world) - where he hides by blending into the crowd.

Richard Smith is clearly heavily influenced by OHMSS. This scene is reminiscent of George Lazenby's Bond trying to blend in at a carnival when Blofeld's goons are after him. The doomed love affair at the heart of Reunion in Death is also very OHMSS.

Bond learns that Michiko's father was the boss of a chemical company that went bankrupt after a spate of suspicious accidents engineered by Nakasone. Michiko's father committed suicide and Nakasone then absorbed the company into his own empire. It was what you might call a hostile takeover! Bond investigates Nakasone further and breaks into Nakasone's fish processing factory. 007 cracks the safe and finds superconductors which were stolen from Sir Robert Grey's company. Bond is discovered and a big fight/chase sequence plays out in which 007 harpoons one goon and throws another in a fish grinding machine.

Bond is eventually captured again and threatened by Nakosone with a railgun. Nakosone also, rather ludicrously, demands to know who helped Bond escape from the castle.

You'd think that he would have worked out by now that his wife had betrayed him! Bond is rescued when Tanaka and his men intervene and a big gun battle breaks out. Bond and Michiko end up hiding in a Buddhist temple and Ryuichi Tanaka is eventually killed trying to help them escape. Bond and Michiko managed to get into a car seemingly belonging to one of Tanaka's men but he turns out to be one of Nakasone's goons and Bond fights him for control of the car.

The out of control car ends up careening down a hill and smashing through a shanty town of flimsy houses. Fans of Hong Kong cinema will note that this sequence is clearly inspired by the superb action packed opening to the brilliant 1985 Jackie Chan film Police Story. There is then a train sequence and the henchman Ng pursues in a helicopter. Ng crashes the helicopter but survives (shades of Richard Kiel's indestructible Jaws). Bond hides out in the British Embassy but Ng infiltrates the embassy in disguise and kills Michiko. Bond returns to London where M has now recuperated. M refuses to grant official permission for Bond to return to Nakasone's castle but accepts that Bond will go anyway.

Bond places explosives around the castle and detonates them and is then confronted by Nakasone. Nakasone is forced to view the destruction on video screens. His henchman Ng arrives and Bond shoots him. Nakasone takes his chance to escape and Bond sets off in pursuit through the fire and destruction of the partially destroyed castle. Nakosone manages to find a samurai suit and sword to use and attacks Bond. The end of the battle comes when Bond throws him off the top of the castle. It transpires that Ng is not dead and survived being shot by Bond because he was wearing a bullet proof vest. Ng attacks Bond but 007 eventually manages to defeat him. Bond detonates the rest of his explosives in order to completely destroy the castle. In the last scene Bond visits the graves of Michiko and Tanaka.

Reunion in Death was said to be a fairly solid and straight laced script that might have suited Timothy Dalton very well.

However, its chances of going before the cameras were slim to say the least. It is doubtful that the producers would have wanted a relatively gloomy third Dalton film that was set almost exclusively in Japan and ended with 007 grieving for the wife of the villain! I suspect they might have wanted to lighten the tone somewhat after Licence To Kill. That said though, Reunion in Death was an admirable attempt to lace more Flemingesque trappings than usual into a Bond script. The treatment is also refreshingly light on gadgets and technology and some of the chase sequences are charmingly old school.

CHAPTER THIRTEEN

After an appearance in the 1993 film Naked in New York, Timothy Dalton made a TV movie called Red Eagle (aka Lie Down with Lions). Red Eagle (which also featured Jürgen Prochnow and Omar Sharif) was a spy drama based on a book by Ken Follett. It was a strangely jarring experience to see Timothy Dalton in such a cheapjack spy film after Daylights and Licence To Kill. Dalton then signed to play Rhett Butler in Scarlett - a TV miniseries sequel to Gone with the Wind. The cast of Scarlett included Sean Bean. Unknown to anyone at the time, Bean was soon to become one of the actors vying to replace Dalton as 007. While on the set of Scarlett, Timothy Dalton read the Michael France Bond 17 draft called Goldeneye. Dalton enjoyed the script and thought it would make a good film. He knew that he needed to make a decision regarding his participation in Bond 17. Things were moving fast and they needed to know if he was in or out.

Timothy Dalton now made the decision not to return as James Bond. Many years later he said that his decision was prompted by the fact that he only wanted to come back and make one more film whereas EON didn't see the point of this. "Cubby Broccoli asked if I would come back," said Dalton, "and I said, 'Well, I've actually changed my mind a little bit. I think that I'd love to do one. Try and take the best of the two that I have done, and consolidate them into a third.' And he said, quite rightly, 'Look, Tim. You can't do one. There's no way, after a five-year gap between movies that you can come back and just do one. You'd have to plan on four or five.' And I thought, oh, no, that would be the rest of my life. Too much. Too long. So I respectfully declined."

In April 1994, Timothy Dalton released a statement confirming the end of his tenure as Bond. 'Even though the producers have always made it clear to me that they want me to resume my role in their next James Bond feature, I have now made this difficult decision. As an actor, I believe it is now time to leave that wonderful image behind and accept the challenge of new ones. The Broccolis have been good to me as producers. They have been more special as friends.' EON released their own statement in which they said - 'We have never thought of anyone but Timothy as the star of the 17th James Bond film. We understand his reasons and we will honor his decision.'

MGM's John Calley was straight out of the gate with his own statement about Timothy Dalton's resignation from the most famous role in cinema. 'While we were sorry to learn of Timothy Dalton's decision regarding the role of James Bond, we are proceeding with the project as planned and will meet our targeted summer 1995 release date.' One could be forgiven for suspecting that Calley was less than sincere when he said MGM were sorry to learn of Dalton's departure! The obvious question, still debated by Bond fans to this day, is the question of whether Dalton jumped of his own free will or was pushed overboard by studio pressure. It's hard to say with absolute certainty one way or the other.

Some have alleged that Dalton was fired but then allowed to release a statement saying he left of his own free will as a courtesy. That though doesn't sound like something Cubby Broccoli would allow to happen. The evidence for this conspiracy theory is sometimes cited as the fact that Dalton was a pallbearer at Cubby's funeral a few years later but never signed any Bond merchandise with an MGM logo. The alleged subtext is presumably that Dalton was loyal to the Broccoli family but had a grudge against MGM. If Dalton was actually fired at the behest of MGM you'd imagine he probably would have spoken about it by now though. Enough time has passed and Dalton is not exactly a shrinking violet.

Another conspiracy that has been floated is the allegation that MGM told EON they would not allocate a third Dalton film a high budget but WOULD sanction a big budget with a new actor. In some versions of this story, MGM pull the nuclear option and say they will not fund a new James Bond film at all if Dalton is involved! While it is true that in such a scenario EON's hands would have been tied (they were obviously in no position to fund and distribute a Bond film on their own) it still doesn't seem very likely that Cubby Broccoli and EON would have participated in any move to throw Timothy Dalton to the sharks.

Most people seem to think that Timothy Dalton's decision to leave was simply a mutual agreement. Dalton felt too much time had passed since Licence To Kill and he didn't want to be tied down to another Bond contract. He was in his late forties now and probably had little desire to throw himself back into the Bond circus again. EON would almost certainly have allowed him to come back if he'd wanted to but perhaps in the end EON, like MGM, were happy to have a fresh slate for was clearly going to be a pivotal film in the franchise. Goldeneye was going to be the first Bond film for six years. The franchise had never endured such a long gap between movies. Would anyone still care about Bond when the new film came out? That was the question EON and MGM must have asked themselves.

In 1994 a $100 million James Cameron action spy film called True Lies was released. True Lies starred Arnold Schwarzenegger as Harry Tasker, a secret agent for a U.S. intelligence agency named Omega Sector. The opening of True Lies has Schwarzenegger emerging from a pond in scuba gear to reveal a white tuxedo underneath like Sean Connery in the Goldfinger PTS. True Lies (though it seems rather dated today and has a draggy subplot involving Jamie Lee Curtis, comic relief from Tom Arnold, and some distinctly un-PC elements) was rather alarming to MGM and EON when it appeared because it was a reminder of the sort of competition they would face. True Lies had spectacular action sequences including a nuclear explosion, Harrier Jump Jet shenanigans, and skyscraper chases on horseback.

The latest draft of the Goldeneye script actually had to be rewritten because of certain similarities to True Lies. It is believed that these changes made Goldeneye leaner and lighter than it had been before. This was not only to avoid story comparisons to True Lies but also to transition the script from Dalton's Bond to a new Bond. The Bond team also decided to make the action bigger in the Goldeneye script for fear of falling behind the times and not competing with movies like True Lies. Goldeneye was not a film that could afford to pussyfoot around or be experimental. It had to hit those classic Bond 'bumps' (as Cubby would say) and hit them with all the force it could muster.

The search for Timothy Dalton's replacement quickly began but it was not to prove the most complex or lengthy task EON had ever faced when it came to finding a new James Bond actor. As ever, a revolving door of young British actors were interviewed or tested. Jason Isaacs, Mark Frankel, Greg Wise, Colin Wells, Jeremy Northam, James Purefoy, Sean Bean, Paul McGann, and Nathaniel Parker were all names mulled over by EON. Another actor on the mind of EON (and also MGM) was Ralph Fiennes - though nothing came of this. "There was a conversation that was great and a meeting with Cubby Broccoli, that was terrific," said Fiennes. "I think that's all I can say, except that it didn't lead to anything on both sides. I don't think I felt ready to commit and I think they were looking at Pierce [Brosnan]." Fiennes would later play M in the Daniel Craig Bond films.

Despite all the interviews and casting calls, a familiar name was always the red hot favourite to take the 007 mantle from Timothy Dalton. Step forward Pierce Brosnan - still only 41 years-old and (here was the REALLY crucial part) acceptable to both EON and MGM. Brosnan didn't even have to audition for the part because EON obviously still had his 1986 screen test in the vault. There was something inevitable about Pierce Brosnan becoming James Bond. It was just something that always seemed destined to happen one day. In May 1994, Brosnan dodged questions linking him to the part of Bond but this was simply misdirection before an official announcement. Brosnan already knew he had the part in the bag.

Pierce Brosnan's only mildly serious rival for Timothy Dalton's tux was said to be Liam Neeson but Neeson wasn't very enthusiastic at all. Neeson said he was heavily 'courted' but ruled himself out of the running. Neeson was about to get married and didn't want to become involved in something as time consuming as making James Bond films. He also had little interest in making action films at the time. Neeson's attitude to appearing in action films would obviously change many years later in the veteran phase of his career. These days Liam Neeson seems to make nothing but action films! I must confess that I never quite understood why Liam Neeson always seemed to be so high on studio lists when it came to Bond. Sure, he's a very fine actor but Neeson never personally struck me as very James Bondian.

In the summer of 1994, in one of the worst kept secrets in the world, Pierce Brosnan was officially announced as the new James Bond. The night before the press conference to announce the new James Bond, Brosnan had been spotted by the media dining in a London restaurant. You probably didn't have to be Hercule Poirot to deduce that Brosnan was in town for the Bond press conference. Brosnan had finally won the part he seemed destined to play from the moment he met Cubby Broccoli on the set of For Your Eyes Only all those years ago. The Bond series had come full circle. Dalton replaced Brosnan and now Brosnan was replacing Dalton.

In the 007 auditions for Goldeneye, Sean Bean impressed the producers enough to secure the consolation prize of rogue Double O villain Alec Trevelyan in the movie. EON brought in Jeffrey Caine and later Kevin Wade to revise the Goldeneye script by Michael France. Bruce Feirstein was then brought in to do a final draft. The rewrites were intended to turn the Goldeneye script from a Dalton film into a Brosnan film. In a rather bold move, John Woo was invited to direct Goldeneye but declined the offer. Martin Campbell was hired as the director in the end and a new era of James Bond was launched in 1995.

Believe it or not, there was actually a lot of scepticism regarding Goldeneye before it was released. When the cast was unveiled, the British press noted the absence of big stars and even suspected that this film was maybe being made on the cheap or something. Nothing could have been further from the actual truth. Goldeneye had a budget of $60 million and was fully committed to reviving the fortunes of the mothballed Bond franchise. Far from hammering the final nail into 007's coffin, Goldeneye sparked a revival in the franchise and made James Bond feel bigger than it had been since the halycon days of Roger Moore battling Jaws in The Spy Who Loved Me and Moonraker.

Goldeneye had two excellent Bond Girls in Famke Janssen and Isabelle Scorupco, a terrific bungee jump opening, a fantastic tank chase, an amazing title sequence by Daniel Kleinman, model work by the great Derek Meddings, a grand scale climax shot at the Arecibo Observatory in Puerto Rico, and plenty of Bondian trappings. Goldeneye also reflected changing times with a female M and reflections on whether Bond might be a dinosaur of the Cold War. Pierce Brosnan proved to be a safe pair of hands as the new James Bond. He was lighter than Timothy Dalton but not as flippant as Roger Moore. Brosnan was somewhere in the middle and seemed to be the right man for the franchise at this potentially tricky juncture. Brosnan lacked the darkness of Timothy Dalton but seemed to be having a lot of fun.

"The fate of the studio (MGM) rested in the hands of James Bond," said John Cork, "and Goldeneye's success would not only confidently state that there was profit to be wrung from future 007 films, but it would drive up the value of the Bond catalog. Goldeneye proved all the doubters wrong. Bond's continued relevance, it turned out, had little to do with Cold War politics or studio equity. It had everything to do with quality. Everyone involved in making Goldeneye was hungry, and it shows. The film is also the introduction of Barbara Broccoli as a key creative voice in the Bond team, the launch of

Pierce Bronsan's career as Bond, and the best evidence that the creative team could take 007 beyond the decades that defined him."

Goldeneye (with the advantage of a fantastic marketing campaign and a November release) was a huge financial success and ensured that the Bond series would survive and be around for many more years to come. That said though, I must confess to a slight tinge of disappointment after I viewed Goldeneye for the first time. I couldn't help thinking that the two Timothy Dalton films were much more interesting and, well, simply better. I remember being disappointed that the end of the PTS had obvious CGI when Bond is in freefall chasing after the plane. It was a sharp contrast to Timothy Dalton doing real stunts. Still, despite my own personal preference for the Dalton era, Goldeneye made much more money than Daylights or Licence To Kill and got better reviews. An obvious question to ask, and it is one that Bond fans still discuss on forums, is what would Goldeneye have been like with Timothy Dalton? Would it have worked with Dalton?

Not all of Goldeneye would have suited Timothy Dalton but the general story and many parts of the film might have served him very well. You can't really imagine Dalton hanging upside down in the toilet during the PTS to deliver a quip like Brosnan does and you can't really see Dalton's Bond suggestively wrestling with Xenia in the sauna. Scenes like this were fine for Brosnan's Bond and he made them funny but you can't see them working for Dalton. The PTS in Goldeneye with the 'nine years later' caption after the titles would have made more sense with Timothy Dalton because we had seen Dalton's Bond in a Cold War adventure back in the 1980s in The Living Daylights.

Dalton would have been fine I think in the playful Aston Martin chase which begins Goldeneye. As for casting in the film, it's debatable that Sean Bean could have played Trevelyan in a Dalton version of Goldeneye. Bean is twelve years younger than Dalton so Trevelyan might have needed to be a little older if Timothy had made the film. You believe that Brosnan's Bond and Bean's 006 are contemporaries of similar age who have been on many missions together but it would have been more difficult to convey this with Dalton and Bean. It's interesting that EON apparently wanted Alan Rickman to play Trevelyan. Rickman would have made a terrific Trevelyan in a Dalton version of Goldeneye.

If Dalton had made Goldeneye it seems logical to presume that Caroline Bliss would have been back as Moneypenny - which would have been fine. I suspect that even if Dalton had come back, EON would still have cast Judi Dench as the new M. What a prospect that would have been. Dalton and Judi Dench together! It would have been like being at the Old Vic. Michael Kitchen as Tanner would have worked very well with Dalton too in Goldeneye. The Russian scenes would, I feel, have served Dalton very well in Goldeneye. One can easily imagine Dalton's Bond in the errie statue park. Generally, not an awful would have had to change to make Goldeneye a Dalton film rather than a Brosnan film.

There are certainly things Brosnan did better than Dalton - like delivering quips and visual humour. I love the moment in Goldeneye where Brosnan's Bond takes out the assailant on the yacht with precise economy and minimal effort and then nonchalantly dabs at his forehead with a towel. This is the sort of thing that Brosnan would always do better than Dalton. It's a very nice little 'Brosnan Bond' moment. However, there are of course things that Dalton does better than Brosnan. I think Dalton probably would have sold the betrayal by Trevelyan better than Brosnan and given this drama in the story more authenticity and impact.

Even though Goldeneye could plausibly have been an excellent film with Timothy Dalton and a profitable hit (I can't believe that with the 'Bond is Back' novelty of the first film in six years, a November release, and a HUGE marketing blitz that a Timothy Dalton led Goldeneye wouldn't have been anything other than a success at the box-office!) one can still understand why the studio were keen to have a new actor playing James Bond by the time the film neared production. The stars just seemed to align for Brosnan in 1995 in a way that they never quite did for Timothy Dalton. Goldeneye even spawned one of the most famous video games of all time with 1997's classic first person shooter Goldeneye 007. This was a wonderful turn of events for EON because it made James Bond a much more visible brand to young people.

After the release of Goldeneye in 1995, the 007 franchise had a 41 year-old Pierce Brosnan ready, willing, and able to make as many Bond films as they wanted him to do. Brosnan absolutely loved playing James Bond. He'd still be making Bond films today if they'd let him! The conclusion of an alternate universe Timothy Dalton version of Goldeneye though would have left the franchise with a 49 year-old leading man who may or may not have wanted to make the next film. While a Timothy Dalton version of Goldeneye would have been a terrific bonus for Dalton Bond fans it clearly made more commercial and forward thinking sense to begin a new era.

In a perfect world without litigation, Goldeneye would have been Dalton's fourth or fifth and final film rather than his mythical never to happen third movie. There are just times in the Bond franchise where the producers must make changes and look to the future. This was why some Bond fans were frustrated when Barbara Broccoli waited around forever for Daniel craig to decide if he wanted to make a fifth film. It basically meant we had to wait years for a film featuring a fiftysomething actor who wouldn't be returning again. It would have made more sense to get the cameras rolling again sooner by launching a new era with a younger actor. You could argue though that Barbara was just being loyal to Craig in the fashion that her father Cubby had been loyal to Dalton all those years ago.

CHAPTER FOURTEEN

As the Bond series enjoyed a new lease of life with Pierce Brosnan, Timothy Dalton threatened to become rather forgotten. He continued to work but few people saw the films he was making at the time. I mean, have you ever watched Salt Water Moose? Has anyone? By the end of the nineties, Dalton seemed to be back in the TV miniseries world he had inhabited before James Bond. The interesting thing about Dalton though was that he aged very well. There's no doubt that he could have made Goldeneye in 1994 and hardly looked a day older than he did in Licence To Kill. It was all academic now though. James Bond was in Dalton's past.

In 1996, Timothy Dalton attended Cubby Broccoli's memorial service and was photographed with Roger Moore and Pierce Brosnan. It was a wonderful image to see these three Bonds all together (sadly, Sean Connery, who always had a more difficult relationship with Cubby because of disputes over money, did not turn up at the service). Timothy Dalton proved to be a dignified and excellent ambassador for the Bond franchise. He attended the 40th anniversary celebrations and also spoke intelligently and respectfully about the franchise in interviews. Dalton said he had no regrets about walking away from 007 in 1994. "I can't possibly miss it, because it is part of my life," said Dalton at the 40th anniversary celebrations. "It is in my blood, it is in my heart, it is part of me, you go on to do other things but you never leave it behind."

In 1995, when Goldeneye was released, Dalton had looked at a big billboard of Brosnan as 007 and felt a sense of relief. Dalton was grateful for the fact that it was Brosnan and not him who now had to do all the interviews, chat shows, and photo shoots to promote the film. Timothy Dalton had a lot in common with Brosnan's successor Daniel Craig. Craig always gave one the impression that he would rather be at the dentist than a press conference and Dalton was cut from a similar cloth. Dalton was a very private person who never craved any limelight. This side of him was happy to walk away from Bond.

In 1996, the maverick Irish film producer Kevin McClory declared in Variety magazine that he had plans to make a renegade Bond film to go up against Pierce Brosnan's second 007 film. "I'm back in the Bond business because I have a couple of films I want to direct and Bond can provide the finance," said McClory. "I didn't want to make another Bond film, but now that I've come this far, I'm enjoying it immensely. The film will be called Warhead 2000 and an actor has been chosen to play Bond. But we won't announce it yet to keep the competition in the dark. No, it's not Sean Connery. He's too old for the part now. But he has said he would play the villain in a James Bond film if the price was right." As ever with Kevin McClory though, there was a huge gulf between his public pronouncements and cold hard reality.

Before the birth of the James Bond franchise by Cubby Broccoli and Harry Saltzman, McClory had worked with Ian Fleming on plans for what would have been the first movie featuring James Bond. The screenplay for this proposed Bond film was called Longitude 78 West. Fleming later used Longitude 78 West as the basis for his novel Thunderball.

All hell broke loose because Fleming didn't give McClory or Jack Whittingham (who had also worked on Longitude 78 West) any credit. The inevitable court case which followed left Kevin McClory with the legal right to make a James Bond film based on Thunderball.

Cubby Broccoli was shrewd in the way that he handled Kevin McClory. He brought McClory in as a producer on EON's film version of Thunderball and made McClory agree not to produce a Thunderball film of his own for at least ten years. Broccoli probably presumed (not unreasonably) the James Bond series wouldn't even be around in ten years. Once the ten years were up though, the Bond series was still around and Kevin McClory set about making his own Bond film. McClory's plans to make a film in the seventies called Warhead were frustrated but his long threatened renegade Bond film finally arrived in 1983 with Never Say Never Again.

The remarkable thing about McClory's plan to make a rival James Bond film in the 1990s is that he was backed by SONY - who were now headed by a certain John Calley! "We are satisfied that McClory has the right to make James Bond," said Calley. MGM were understandably furious that Calley, who obviously had insider knowledge on the Bond films, was now apparently plotting against the official Bond franchise. Roland Emmerich and Dean Devlin, the team behind Independence Day and Godzilla, were supposedly working on the new renegade James Bond film according to media reports.

McClory's new Bond film was alleged to involve a plot in which Blofeld hijacks ships in the Bermuda Triangle to steal nuclear weapons. The media widely reported that Liam Neeson and Timothy Dalton were vying to play James Bond in the movie and that Sean Connery was in talks to play the villain. It's safe to say that none of this was verifiable and about as likely to happen as Eddie Edwards winning a ski-jump gold medal. Kevin McClory, who was amusingly called the "Rip Van Winkle of copyright laws" by MGM in the court case, eventually lost his legal battle to make another Bond film and SONY eventually threw the towel in. The legal wrangles had a nice bonus for EON as they ended up with the rights to Casino Royale (the one Fleming novel that had eluded them).

Kevin McClory had mentioned Timothy Dalton as someone he was interested in when it came to James Bond candidates for his Warhead film. The chances of this happening were less than zero. Not only had Timothy Dalton moved on from Bond but he was also friends with the Broccoli family. There is no way Dalton would have been disloyal to EON and the Broccolis by appearing in a rival James Bond film. The strange headlines concerning Warhead in the late 1990s were a reminder that no one can ever completely escape from the shadow of James Bond once they have played the part. This was certainly the case with Timothy Dalton and all the dubious headlines linking him to Kevin McClory.

Happily, despite the fact that his career seemed to stagnate in the late 1990s, Timothy Dalton was never really forgotten in the end. The cult status of Flash Gordon continued to escalate and he spoofed his Bond image in Looney Tunes - Back in Action. He won new audiences through Toy Story and Edgar Wright's Hot Fuzz. He even appeared in Doctor Who. Dalton was also the lead of the prestige cult show Penny Dreadful and maintained a high profile when he was cast in Doom Patrol. Dalton became something of a national treasure in the end. Best of all was the fact that his two Bond films became somewhat cultish. It seemed to take an awfully long time but in the end people finally started to appreciate what Dalton brought to Bond and what he had tried to do with Daylights and Licence To Kill.

Although the Pierce Brosnan era started very well with Goldeneye, it rather flattered to decieve in the end. Tomorrow Never Dies was very entertaining (with an excellent performance by Brosnan) but strangely forgettable all the same while The World Is Not Enough, the PTS aside, was rather average. As for Die Another Day, well that is a book in and of itself. Die Another Die quickly became one of the most reviled films (though it actually made a lot of money and got decent reviews) in Bond history with its invisible Aston Martin, CGI parasurfing (which looked like a cut scene from an MSDOS game), Toby Stephens in a Robocop suit, and Madonna fencing cameo. Die Another Day, the 40th anniversary Bond movie, was supposed to be Brosnan's The Spy Who Loved Me but it obviously didn't quite pan out that way. Lewis Gilbert and Cubby Broccoli could have made Die Another Day a fantastic Bond movie but Lee Tamahori and Barbara Broccoli most assuredly could not.

The Brosnan films are generally felt to have been somewhat less than the sum of their parts. The writing was not great and the choices for director were not the most radical or exciting. The Brosnan films felt slightly too safe in the end. They made one yearn for the harder edge of the Dalton pictures. Compare, for example, Licence To Kill with Die Another Day. The contrast is amazing. It was Die Another Day that made Barbara Broccoli and Michael G. Wilson feel like they wanted to start all over again and reboot the franchise. They wanted to make the Bond films more serious and harder edged again. The decision to do this was tremendously successful when Casino Royale came out in 2006.

It was all down to timing (and our old friend marketing). In 2006, people were patently more accepting of a mainstream blockbuster with a gloomy or downbeat aura. They were more receptive to a Bond film that took itself seriously (in so far as a Bond film can be serious - you wouldn't really say that any James Bond film was in the least bit realistic). It was sort of unfair really that when Casino Royale came out everyone (excluding Bond fans of course - they were well aware of Dalton) wrote as if Daniel Craig was the first person to take James Bond seriously and doing any acting in the role. Timothy Dalton was, in hindsight, simply well ahead of his time. Nearly two decades to be precise!

The fine balance when it comes to perceptions of the cinematic Bond was illustrated when Daniel Craig's second film Quantum of Solace was roasted by critics and Bond fans (though I'm sure the film has its defenders in the Bond fandom community) for being too dour and joyless. Even the likes of John Glen and Lewis Gilbert chimed in to say that didn't think Quantum of Solace was a Bond film. One film in and the hard edged serious Bond concept had already outstayed its welcome! I'm being flippant as Casino Royale was clearly a better film than Quantum and the Craig era regained its footing with Skyfall but it was evidence nonetheless of how tricky it is to have clarity of purpose in a Bond tenure and how it is impossible to always please everyone.

The Brosnan films could never quite decide at times if they wanted Pierce to be Timothy Dalton or Roger Moore. Angst felt out of place in the Brosnan era too whenever they tried to slip some in. A few times they tried to give Brosnan a small reflective moment where we are supposed to see how difficult it must be to have his job as a secret agent assassin but it just doesn't suit Brosnan's Bond. Brosnan's Bond feels like someone who loves having a licence to kill and roaming around the world! You feel like Brosnan should be in Connery or Moore style fantastical epics like You Only Live Twice or The Spy Who Loved Me - not trying to make Bond human.

By contrast, when the Daniel Craig films made an overt attempt to inject slightly more humour and old school Bond tongue-in-cheekery in Spectre it didn't quite seem to suit him. The two Timothy Dalton films, in retrospect, seem amazingly comfortable in their own skin and single minded in concept. The two Dalton films seek to make Bond less flippant and seem more like a real person. The end results might not have been everyone's cup of tea but they have an admirable clarity of purpose. I personally find the two Timothy Dalton films more rewatchable any of the Daniel Craig films. I still have fun whenever I watch The Living Daylights and Licence To Kill. While the Daniel Craig films are obviously well made and well acted, they don't have that same fun factor which makes me want to return again and again.

Looking back now, it's easy to underestimate how radical Timothy Dalton's Bond was at the time. To go from something like Octopussy to Licence To Kill in the space of a few films is pretty amazing when you think about it. It was a brave decision to cast a Shakespearean stage actor as James Bond and give him sufficient elbow room to craft his own interpretation. It would probably be fair to say that Dalton never quite completely clicked with casual audiences and will never go down as the most popular Bond but his tenure has rightfully earned fresh retrospective plaudits in recent years.

One thing I never quite understand is why The Living Daylights and Licence To Kill are often ranked so low in James Bond lists and rankings. These two films are, I feel, fascinating entries in the eclectic broad sweep of the Bond franchise and mostly excellent in their own right. Daylights and Licence To Kill are fascinating because they genuinely feel as if they are trying to do something new. They feel less formula bound and more surprising than many Bond films. Take Daylights for example - when you watch the film for the first time it is difficult at first to work out if the movie even has a villain. Was this ambiguity deliberate? The romance between Klara and Bond is incredibly low-key for the franchise and Bond actually has to earn Klara's trust. Elements like these were quite refreshing at the time.

Timothy Dalton in The Living Daylights feels like a more convincing spy than most of the Bond actors. Take for example the briefing at the Blayden safe house. Dalton is in the background smoking and silently looking on with his intense wolfish eyes. He's completely James Bond. You genuinely believe that he is an intelligence agent. Accusations that Dalton's Bond is completely humourless seem unfair because he is fairly easygoing in parts of The Living Daylights. I suspect that those who remember Dalton as being humourless in the part are thinking almost exclusively of Licence To Kill. It is true that Dalton is rather grim in Licence To Kill at times but Bond is on a revenge mission for Felix and Della so you wouldn't really expect him to be a barrel of laughs in this story.

Timothy Dalton had obviously read the Fleming novels himself and noticed that humour is thin on the ground in comparison to the Bond movie franchise. Dalton presumably felt then that toning down the japery and quips was being faithful to Ian Fleming. You could argue though that the balance between Fleming's Bond and the Cinematic Bond was not judged perfectly in Licence To Kill. Dalton seemed to acknowledge this himself in an interview where he said that he'd have liked a little more humour in Licence To Kill. You'd imagine the balance would have been better in any third Dalton film - a fact which makes the absence of Dalton's third Bond picture all the more frustrating.

The praise which greeted Casino Royale in 2006 must have been noted with a wry smile by Dalton. In 2006, you might venture, they sort of embraced what Dalton had tried to do with the character in the late 1980s. 'The globetrotting espionage antics of Dalton's 007 were depicted in a much more realistic manner than the average Bond plot,' wrote GamesRadar. 'Casino Royale would later be lauded for grounding the Bond franchise in gritty realism, but the short-lived Dalton era already did that. Dalton's Bond acted on his own authority, following his own judgment, which resulted in more morally challenging stories than fans were accustomed to. Dalton did a lot of his own stunts – unlike Moore, whose stunt doubles could be spotted from a mile away – and his love interests had a lot more agency than the average Bond girls. None of the romantic scenes in Dalton's movies have the problematic overtones that most of the other movies do, because his Bond was actually interested in connecting with women instead of objectifying them.'

Casual retrospectives of the Bond franchise can sometimes be rather lazy and predictable. Roger Moore, for example, is inevitably trashed in such pieces. And yet, there would be no James Bond franchise today were it not for Roger Moore. Moore achieved something quite miraculous in the way that he showed the franchise could be still be viable and go on and on even without Sean Connery. Roger Moore is an impressively witty, suave and charismatic James Bond in films like The Spy Who Loved Me. Who else but Roger Moore could have kept his head above water in the lavish madness of Moonraker? Retrospectives also tend to gloss over George Lazenby in equally dismissive fashion. They'll acknowledge that OHMSS was a very good film but give one the impression that Lazenby was useless. Well, hold on a minute. Lazenby wasn't useless. He was pretty good all things considered. The final scene, when Bond is a broken man after the murder of Diana Rigg's Tracy, is played amazingly well by Lazenby.

All of the Bond actors have contributed to the franchise and brought their own specific traits and unique interpretations.

The franchise is richer for this. It's lazy to dismiss any Bond actor as if they were hopeless because this has never been the case. Timothy Dalton got his unfair share of brickbats in lazy Bond retrospectives for years but I sense the tide has slightly turned on Dalton's Bond over time. Dalton has at least received some overdue credit for the changes he tried to implement. Dalton has always been appreciated in Bond fandom though. It would probably be reasonable to say that Timothy Dalton was always more appreciated by Bond fans than casual audiences.

'Timothy Dalton is a Bond with substance,' wrote the FlixChatter Film Blog in 2014 in an article about Licence To Kill, 'bad-ass but refined, gritty without being thuggish and he can be menacing and vulnerable in a matter of seconds. Case in point, when Bond confronts Pam Bouvier in the hotel room, he was angry enough to pull the trigger on her, but when she reveals the truth that 'there's more to it than his personal vendetta,' Dalton's expression immediately immediately softens and the remorse is palpable on his face as he hands her gun back to her. Nice to see the glamorous playboy actually fights out of love and loyalty and the story utilizes Dalton's Shakespearean training perfectly. He's not a super spy that people can't relate to, but he's plays Bond as a human being with real angst and real feelings, but as it's said in the poster, he's got a real dangerous side to him that is both intimidating and sexy. He's believably ruthless, too, as when he threatened a beautiful woman "Make a sound, and you're dead!" we believe that he actually could pull the trigger. The tall and lean Dalton is both a physical and cerebral Bond and he has that understated swagger that effective but isn't showy.'

The James Bond franchise is one of those pop culture monuments that everyone seems to have an opinion about. As long as people continue to debate eras, actors, and films both old and new then the franchise can feel secure in its relevance and future. It shows that people still care. When they bring Bond down to earth some people will complain that the franchise has become too dour and humourless. When they go for humour or the fantastical, some people will complain that it's become a cartoon parody. You can't please everyone. All you can do is hope you've pleased a majority of people. The Holy Grail for the Bond franchise is to find the right balance of humour, action, and drama in each movie. Sometimes they manage to do this and sometimes they don't.

Retrospectives which have dismissed the Timothy Dalton era as a misfire or failure tend to forget that both Dalton and The Living Daylights were well received in 1987. Licence To Kill's reviews were hardly disastrous either. For what it's worth, Licence To kill has a higher Rotten Tomatoes rating than Quantum of Solace or Spectre and a higher rating than the last three Brosnan films. Of the Brosnan era, only Goldeneye outscores Licence To Kill on RT and that's only by 1%. The problem for Timothy Dalton was that he didn't get to consolidate his interpretation of Bond with a third film. There is therefore a lazy assumption to assume he must have been a failure because he only appeared in two films. As we have seen though, the relative brevity of his tenure was down to litigation. Were it not for the litigation we would almost certainly have got a third and fourth Dalton film in the early 1990s. If he had made four films then the perception of Timothy Dalton would be completely different.

I think an obvious factor in my fondness for the Timothy Dalton films now is nostalgia. The two Dalton films were the last Bond movies produced by Cubby Broccoli. They were the last to have a Maurice Binder title sequence. Timothy Dalton was the last Bond actor to have John Barry score one of his films. He was the last Bond actor to have a Richard Maibaum script or Robert Brown as M. Dalton was the last James Bond who was briefed through those leather padded doors at Universal Exports rather than the drab MI6 building at Vauxhall Cross. For all these reasons and more, I find the Dalton films cosy and nostalgic now. To me they simply have more charm than the Bond films that followed. Timothy Dalton can be proud of his contribution to the Bond franchise. He brought something new to the part and did it his way. In the end that's all you can really ask of any Bond actor.